From Marcus

Christmas 1984.

Dancer
Men in Dance

Mary Clarke and Clement Crisp

Dancer
Men in Dance

BRITISH BROADCASTING CORPORATION

Title-page photograph: Patrick Harding-Irmer of the London Contemporary Dance Theatre

Published by the British Broadcasting Corporation
35 Marylebone High Street, London W1M 4AA

ISBN 0 563 20261 0

First published 1984

Set in 12/15 Monophoto Bembo
and printed in England by BAS Printers Limited,
Over Wallop, Stockbridge, Hampshire

Contents

We dedicate this book to Sam B. Montgomery
with affection and gratitude

We would like to express our gratitude to Dr Selma Jeanne Cohen, eminent colleague and friend, for permission to reproduce material from her invaluable series of *Dance Perspectives*; to Lincoln Kirstein we, like the dance in the 20th century, are for ever indebted; to Ann Barzel, distinguished critic, our thanks are also due for permission to quote and also to Erik Aschengreen whose writings on Bournonville are so illuminating.

In preparing this book we are much indebted to Stephen Davies, our editor, and to Linda Blakemore, our designer, and to Julia Matheson and Heather McCubbin of the BBC TV Music and Arts Department we owe a great deal for their care and help, and to Desmond Green our great appreciation of his tireless work in finding pictures.

Mary Clarke, Clement Crisp

Introduction

I recall, too, my adolescent agreement with the local doctor who capped his anti-Soviet diatribe with the statement that 'Communism can't last; any country where men are ballet-dancers and women are doctors is perverted, and going to fall like Rome'.

Ray L. Birdwhistell, *Dance Perspectives: No. 40*

This book is about men as dancers in the theatre. From its origins in the court entertainments of the Renaissance, theatrical dancing was first concerned with the man – the prince, the monarch, the nobleman – as the central figure. The early history of theatre dance is really the history of the *danseur*. It is only with the emergence of Romanticism in ballet during the 1830s that the ballerina becomes the central figure and ultimately the justification for ballet, with the man reduced to a sometimes ignoble and almost invisible role as support for the female dancer. It was the arrival of the Diaghilev company in the first decade of this century which reminded Western Europe that male dancing could be artistically valid and theatrically exciting. Even so it took many years for the idea of dancing as a career for a man to be accepted in the West. The Diaghilev Ballet Russe established a certain mystique about male dancing – it was proper for a Russian man (or a man with a Russian stage name) to dance professionally; it took many more years for the idea of dancing as a career for an ordinary chap to gain any sort of credence. It is in no small part due to the propaganda effect of American modern dance, and the emergence of contemporary dance as an educational force, that prejudice was broken down.

We write as critics who have been observing dance for over forty years. In that time one of the most important developments we have seen is the acceptance of the idea of dancing as a manly pursuit. We would attribute this to several causes: to the increased popularity of ballet and the greater number of performing ensembles; to the great strides made by contemporary dance as an entertainment in the theatre; and not least to the exceptional star quality of such dancers as Rudolf Nureyev and Mikhail Baryshnikov, who have had so profound an effect upon public interest in ballet and have reached beyond the narrow confines of the ballet world to a vaster public. In the central matter of financial reward, there has been a welcome change in monetary prospects for the male dancer. With a more general acceptance of ballet and modern dance there has come more realistic commercial recompense. Allied to this is the fact that for boys there is the possibility of sound technical training from an early age in state schools, which has meant that recruitment of young would-be dancers has boomed, and such schools as the Royal Ballet School, the School of the Paris Opéra, and the School of American Ballet can be selective in their intake of youngsters, while it is usually possible for grants and scholarships to be obtained to secure the boy's training, and for the graduate student to be assured of work thereafter. (Ironically, the same does not obtain always for the girl students: there are today far too many talented women dancers chasing all too few jobs.)

The popularity of the male dancer in the cinema, from Fred Astaire to John Travolta, has gradually conditioned the public into the acceptance of the idea of men dancing. The willingness of many American young men to dance in the contemporary style (and the high standard of male dancing in American musicals) has done much also to change the attitude of teenagers towards dancing. Most recently the pioneer work done in dance as an educational tool, and the enthusiasm for popular dancing reflected by the film *Saturday Night Fever*, have shown the eagerness of the young to dance in clubs and discos with untiring energy. Dance for many of the young has become both a release and a form of self expression, witness the success of *Fame*, and the dance-craze for 'Breaking' and 'Slamming'. It is this enjoyment in, and identification with, dance which is one of the most exhilarating aspects of the male dance scene in ballet, in contemporary dance and in the social dance of our time.

Of course the old myths and prejudices still exist; the very word 'ballet' causes some hackles to rise. The BBC television series to which this book is related will serve to show, though, that the art of the male dancer is concerned with physical strength and physical stamina as well as with the refinements that clothe those essential qualities, and that the male dancer must encompass dramatic and emotional powers quite as serious and important as his muscular skills. Perhaps the best reassurance about male dancing for the general public comes in a comment from *The Ultimate Athlete* by George Leonard which was quoted by James A. Michener in *Sports in America*. 'I can't say that the dancer is the Ultimate Athlete. I am quite certain, however, that the Ultimate Athlete is a dancer.'

Il Ballarino: the Dancer in History

Men are by nature more active than women, and from earliest time dancing was a male prerogative. Even today popular dancing, from the Congo to the Cotswolds, from the Trepack to the Twist, is a man's affair. It is due to historical chance that in ballet women have been more prominent. Ballet grew up with a rush at the height of the nineteenth century Romantic movement, with its emphasis on unearthly mystery, sentiment and moonlit unreality – qualities most fit for female expression. In this century the balance has slowly been righted; some of the most famous dancers have been men. It is no use their being frail and artistic. They must above all be strong, quick supple and rhythmical – the qualities that make a good hurdler or swimmer.

Alexander Bland, *The Dancer's World* (1963 : Collins, London)

Dancing is one of the basics of human behaviour. It is recognised as the most immediate form for expressing emotion, and in primitive societies the dance of the community has always marked the seasons of the year and the seasons of men's lives. In the ancient world dance was a means of worship, and from dance rituals there emerged the first forms of theatre. And though both men and women, as we infer from the earliest pictorial and written records and as we note from the activities of every primitive community, were dancers, it was the man who played the dominant role. Historically, dancing was a manly skill, and with the emergence of many forms of theatrical or religious dance it was a manly art. Our concern in this book is with the male dancer in the Western theatrical tradition, and we cannot better indicate the importance of a man's dancing skills than by quoting from a book published in 1641. Monsieur de Saint Hubert was a gentleman of the court of Louis XIII of France. In 1641 he published a small treatise, *La Manière de Composer et Faire Réussir les Ballets* (*How to Compose a Successful Ballet*) in which he set down the rules for the preparation and presentation of those entertainments which were so fashionable in all the courts of Europe. The *ballets de cour* of the sixteenth and seventeenth centuries were one of the aspects of aristocratic life which tell us so much about the life of the court and the moral and social attitudes of the Renaissance. Court entertainments – dances, joustings, horse ballets (in which gorgeously-caparisoned horses and their no less gorgeously-caparisoned riders paced out elaborate patterns of movement), triumphal entries, firework displays and banquetings – were all part of the panoply of princely living. They stressed the male courtier as chief performer, and involved the greatest in the land, with the monarch often as the central figure.

Monsieur de Saint Hubert observes: 'Everyone knows that, for the young nobleman to be polished, he must learn how to ride, to fence, and to dance. The first skill increases his dexterity, the second his courage, and the last his grace and disposition. Each of these exercises being useful at an appropriate time, one can say that they are of equal value, since Mars is no less the god of war when resting on Venus' bosom than when thundering in the midst of battles. And even kings, princes and noblemen enjoy this divertissement;

Ballerini Milanesi del 1580., che danzano la gagliarda, cavati dall'Opera di Cesare de' Negri Celebre Maestro e scrittore di Ballo in Milano Cagnoni

Renaissance gentlemen were expected to dance well, and the Italian dancing masters were men of considerable social significance: they both polished the courtiers' dance style and devised fresh dances. To aid them in this task they produced dance manuals which are an illuminating picture of manners for their time. Cesare Negri was born in 1530 in Milan and became one of the chief dancing masters of his age, an important enough figure to have danced on a warship in Malta harbour after the battle of Lepanto. In 1604 his *Nuove Inventioni di Balli* was published in Milan. The title-page describes him as 'a famous and excellent professor of dancing' and the book's illustrations, one of which we reproduce here, give a good indication of the correct style and elegance of manner required of a dancing gentleman at the beginning of the seventeenth century. In social dancing and in court entertainments step and style were the same, the court ballets merely offering a more elaborate framework and some dramatic colouring for the dances that were enjoyed in social gatherings.

it must be praiseworthy and, this being so, I decided to express my opinion, which will be shared by those who approve of it; and as to the others, who do things which are not worth while, they will do as they like'. (Dance Perspectives No. 20.)

It is this tradition of the noble male performer which lies at the basis of male dancing during the succeeding centuries. From the earliest days of the Renaissance dancing masters had been important in court life as arbiters of elegance and as guides to aristocratic physical behaviour. The dance manuals surviving from the fifteenth century are clear indications of this, and a work like Caroso's *Il Ballarino* of 1581 is an early example of the care which was taken to prepare the court gentleman as a dancer. The golden age of the court ballet in France came during the reign of King Louis XIV, himself an outstanding dancer whose title of 'Le Roi Soleil' came from his appearance as the Sun God in a *ballet de cour*.

The King offered patronage and support to dancing masters, and it was during his reign that we see the gradual emergence of dance as a theatrical spectacle rather than as court entertainment and activity. The foundation of a royal academy for the presentation of opera-ballets – theatrical performance which combined sung narrative with danced illustration – and the establishment of a school to train professional dancers for these entertainments, is the beginning of the tradition which was to develop into the theatrical dance that we know today as classical ballet.

The French ballet de cour involved the greatest figures at the court. In 1625 an especially brilliant entertainment was staged in the Palace of the Louvre, the king's official residence. This was *Le Ballet des Fées des Forests de St Germain*, whose intention was to describe the qualities most sought-after in a courtier: skill in battle and in the arts, in games and in deportment, and in resisting temptation. The form of a ballet de cour was a series of entrées – dances on a theme – in which the performers were dressed to suggest the physical or spiritual qualities of the character they represented; and these entrées were followed by a final grand ballet in which all the performers and members of their audience might join. This illustration shows King Louis XIII, then in his twenty-fourth year, as 'a Spanish dancer and guitar player' in the first entrée. The splendour of his costuming conveys the undoubted extravagance which went into the presentation of the ballet de cour, and was in itself a representation of royal importance and the grandeur of his very presence.

The Sun King. Louis XIV earned his nickname from his early appearance in court ballets. The political importance of these as statements about the monarch's identity was such that the aristocratic audience understood exactly the aspect of the royal persona which was being proposed by the dances. In *Le Ballet Royal de la Nuit* the King was the Sun, source of light and power, and the young Louis XIV (a notably fine dancer even by court standards) assumed the sun's attributes in effect when he became master of his kingdom. The final part of *Le Ballet Royal de la Nuit*, which took place in the Louvre on 23 February 1653, showed the fifteen-year-old king surrounded by the spirits of Honour, Grace, Love, Valour, Victory, Favour, Renown and Peace – all impersonated by great noblemen – who paid homage to him. The political and allegorical message was clear for all to understand.

Louis XIV in full magnificence in a horse ballet, the *Carrousel* of 1662, which was staged to celebrate the birth of the Dauphin, the heir to the throne. The greatest gentlemen of the court appeared in the five 'quadrilles' – squadrons of horsemen representing Americans, Turks, Persians, Indians and, as here, Romans.

DANSE GENERALE, ET DERNIERE

The *Ballet de la Délivrance de Renaud* of 1617 was a particularly significant political ballet in that it was intended to stress the intentions of the young king Louis XIII to fulfil his duties and to exercise his authority as monarch. To this end an elaborate and splendid court ballet was devised, taking its theme from Tasso's *Jerusalem Delivered*. Its final scene was a general dance in which, to quote Margaret McGowan's definitive study of French court ballet, *L'Art du Ballet de Cour en France*, 'among so many able dancers the King shines through the majesty of his steps. The dance is the mirror of his royal soul.' This illustration comes from the published libretto and shows the court gentlemen in this final dance.

Jean Ballon was born in Paris in 1676 and he died there in 1739. He was famous for his lightness as a dancer, but more significantly for us this engraving conveys both the extreme elegance of dress which was usual for a male dancer and also the elegance of manner : the male dancer was still performing in the image of the aristocrat, although by now dance had entered the theatre and had become the province of professionals like Ballon. The male dancer's ability to perform virtuoso steps is suggested by the complete freedom of legs and feet.

One of the finest English dancing manuals of the eighteenth century is Kellom Tomlinson's *The Art of Dancing Explained by Reading and Figures*, published in London in 1735. Tomlinson, an outstanding dancing master of his time, illustrated his treatise with a series of superb plates which showed the floor plan of the dance, with immaculately drawn figures to indicate correct posture and stance. Each of the plates was dedicated to members of the gentry who were very probably Tomlinson's pupils. The man's freedom to move is in marked contrast to that of the woman, who is still encumbered by her voluminous skirts. These dancers above, shown in a Minuet, are essentially noble amateurs, though elegance of deportment is still essential for them. In the theatre women were by this time acquiring a certain freedom of movement as the first shortening of skirts to mid-calf had taken place. The same quality of genteel style was, however, required from both amateurs and professionals.

Although the first professional female dancers were seen in France in 1681, theatrical dancing was pre-eminently a masculine activity and the male dancer took as his model the aristocratic manners and deportment of the court. Thus the professional male dancer was admired for his elegance and distinction, and the French 'serious' style of dancing, known also as the 'noble' style, was characterised by a princely refinement which may still be traced in the great *danseurs nobles* of today.

So great was the distinction and public appeal of the male dancers in the succeeding years that Louis Dupré (1697–1774) would be referred to by his public as Le Grand Dupré and be nicknamed the God of the Dance. He was an exceptionally handsome man, whose performances were distinguished by their grandeur and nobility of bearing, and even at the age of sixty he was still treading the stage to unqualified public admiration. He was succeeded both as first dancer at the Paris Opéra and as 'God of the Dance' by his pupil, the Italian-born Gaetano Vestris (1729–1808.)

Quarrelsome, vain, a notorious womaniser – like many of the male dancers about whom we have testimony at this time – Gaetano Vestris peacocked his way round Europe exciting the sort of hero worship which was later to be accorded to Nijinsky and Nureyev. His vanity was a byword. When a woman accidentally trod on his foot, he rejected her apologies with the crushing retort: 'You have quite simply put all Paris in mourning for a fortnight.' And when eventually he launched the career of his illegitimate son, Auguste Vestris, he observed that God had given his son the advantage of Gaetano Vestris as his father – something which Nature had denied Gaetano himself.

Left: Gaetano Vestris, 'the god of the dance', is shown in Noverre's ballet *Jason and Medea* at the King's Theatre, London, in 1781. Vestris is wearing the conventional costuming of a 'noble' dancer of the period, for no matter what the ballet's theme, the danseur appeared in the traditional finery of the male star of his day.

Above: Auguste Vestris was dancing in London at the same time as his father in 1781, and this satirical but very attractive engraving shows the young virtuoso at his most exuberant. The younger Vestris's costume indicates the greater freedom in step and in behaviour that was allowed to a dancer in the demi-caractère style: unlike his father, trapped in the dated conventions of the 'noble' or 'serious' manner, Auguste can kick out with joyous abandon. We sense in this engraving by Bartolozzi of a drawing by Nathanial Dance something of the charm of the twenty-one-year-old danseur.

In the ballets of the mid-eighteenth century, at a time when technical beauty of execution and grandeur of bearing were the qualities most sought after, Gaetano Vestris represented the apogee of the dance, and when he and his son appeared in London together a debate in Parliament was cancelled so that MPs might see this illustrious couple. Auguste inherited his father's vanity ('There are only three great men in Europe: the King of Prussia, Monsieur de Voltaire and myself.') and also his title as *Dieu de la Danse*, though his style differed from that of Gaetano, being more brilliant and vivid.

Eighteenth-century male dance was divided into three categories: the *noble* style demanded both physical distinction and height for the impersonation of heroic figures, a reminder of its roots in courtly dance of the Renaissance; the *demi-caractère* style was more obviously sparkling and was entrusted to dancers of smaller stature; the *comique* style was often acrobatic and sometimes vulgar, and demanded less technical finesse. Auguste, with his darting brilliance, was an example of the *demi-caractère* manner. His alert dramatic style and his pirouettes were a sign of the developing physical virtuosity associated with the male dancer at this time. Like his father, he was admired throughout

Europe, and at the cessation of his professional dancing career he became one of the chief teachers in Paris. And it is there that he shaped the talents of two other great male dancers: Auguste Bournonville and Jules Perrot, who were to be very significant choreographers of the Romantic age.

The eighteenth century had seen the emergence of professional female dancers as important figures in the ballet theatre. The very fact of social dress, and the conventions of costuming in the theatre, had meant that female dancers were originally far more constrained in performance than men. And they were not less constrained by reason of the size of their skirts and the elaboration of headdress than by the social image of woman in the eighteeenth century. As theatrical costuming became lighter, female technique developed, but it was not until the French Revolution and the emergence of a radically different style of dress that the female body was liberated for stage dancing. As we enter the nineteenth century we note the increasing advances made in female technique which will presage the appearance of Maria Taglioni and the divinities of the Romantic age, and the subsequent dominance of the ballerina in the theatre.

Left: This illustration formed the frontispiece to the treatise on dancing published in London in 1772 by Giovanni Andrea Gallini, who became Sir John Gallini. It shows, we suppose, the author in the tremendous outfit of a male dancer of the noble style in the theatre. He is wearing the *tonnelet*, that hooped skirt which could extend to arms' width that was customary wear for a male dancer at this time (and which flapped up and down when the dancer leaped) and ribbons, feathers and other accoutrements. This is in effect the last gasp of eighteenth-century dress in the theatre. The French Revolution and the Napoleonic wars would soon sweep this image of the male dancer into oblivion.

Thirty years after the picture of Gallini, the German artist Gottfried Schadow drew this portrait of Salvatore Viganò, the Italian-born dancer and choreographer, and his beautiful Spanish wife Maria Medina in 1800. The complication of dancers' dress of a generation before has now been replaced by more elegantly free clothing, a reflection of the liberation in social dress brought about by the French Revolution. Greater physical freedom for women as for men was to accentuate the move towards greater technical virtuosity.

Carlo Blasis (1797–1878) was one of the great pedagogues in the history of ballet. He did much to lay down and organise the rules underlining classical ballet training, and his precepts remain valid today. These illustrations from his first book, *The Elementary Treatise* of 1820, indicate something of the qualities then required of a male dancer: good stance, turn out from the hip, clean extension of the limbs. The ideas implicit in this training are the substructure to male dancing, and if they were not always revealed in the theatre they were honoured and sought in the classroom throughout the nineteenth century.

Jules Perrot (1810–1892) as he appeared in the ballet *Nathalie* at the Paris Opéra. The scene was set in Switzerland, the heroine was Maria Taglioni as a farmer's daughter, and Perrot looks far more charming in this portrait than contemporary chroniclers would allow. He had started his career as a child performer in grotesque roles in his native Lyon, and when he arrived in Paris to work with Auguste Vestris the old master had, with the wisdom that great teachers pass on to their best pupils, advised him to keep ever on the move on stage. 'Never stay still. Jump about, turn, move around, but never give the public time to look at you closely.' There resulted a technique prodigious enough to shine as brightly as Taglioni's, much to the ballerina's annoyance. Perrot's greater importance, though, was to be a choreographer in the 1840s and 1850s. Above : Perrot in 1875 towards the end of his life, drawn by Degas in class at the Paris Opéra. He is one of the few male figures from the world of dance to be found in Degas' great catalogue of dance portraiture.

The Romantic age, which can be conveniently dated in ballet from the appearance of Maria Taglioni in *La Sylphide* in 1832, marks the beginning of the decline in male dancing. Although male dancing still persisted in the theatre, and Jules Perrot – as dancer and then as choreographer – maintained something of a balance between the sexes, the stage was filling with moonlight and the drifting tarlatans of the goddesses of the Romantic age. As the first true ballerinas captured the imagination of the public and reflected the new concern with fantasy and far-off lands of dream and heightened passions, the male dancer was doomed. The French poet and critic Théophile Gautier, the true voice of Romanticism in his criticisms and commentaries upon ballet at this time, thought the art was concerned with 'physical pleasure and feminine beauty'. He thought male dancers 'monstrous and indecent' and could declare, 'Nothing is indeed more abominable than a man displaying his red neck, his thick muscular arms, and legs with calves like a parish beadle's, while his whole heavy, virile frame shudders with his leaps and pirouettes.'

Thus was announced the attitude which would effectively banish the male dancer from any valid participation in ballet in most western theatres. The most honourable exception is that shown by Auguste Bournonville, who took his elegant French training – fruit of four years' work in Paris with Auguste Vestris – back to Copenhagen in 1830 and there set about the building of a company, a school and a repertory during the next forty-seven years. In all his ballets Bournonville maintained that proper balance between male and female dancing which was neglected throughout the rest of Europe. The great list of his creations – some of which survive today – shows his concern for dramatic liveliness and for the dignity of the male dancer. That today Danish male dancers are among the finest in the world is a direct result of Bournonville's pride in being a fine dancer himself, and his love for a career which he called 'the finest in the world'. It is significant to note, too, that Bournonville was determined that his female dancers should be considered as respectable members of society, at a time when they were in most centres of ballet – notably Paris – thought of as morally reprehensible and fodder for the members of the Jockey Club.

Ballet itself went into a decline in the theatres of Europe as the nineteenth century progressed, and more and more it came to be viewed as little more than an interlude or an adjunct to opera. Even in Paris, where it was preserved in an increasingly ignominious form, it offered no real opportunities for the male dancer, whose role as hero in ballets was sometimes supplanted by a pretty girl *en travesti* (the 'heroes' of *Coppélia* and of *Les Deux Pigeons* were both created by women, and this tradition persisted well into the twentieth century). Elsewhere ballet sank to often disreputable status, being associated mainly with music halls and with the most unambitious sort of spectacle. The male dancer's status was, indeed, so ambiguous in Paris by the 1890s that a motion was seriously proposed in the French Chamber of Deputies to abolish 'these men who display their callipygous charms on stage' and replace them with 'omnibus-conductors, who could be given a pair of tights and three or four francs an evening to enable them to hold up the *danseuses*.'

Maria Taglioni and Antonio Guerra in *L'Ombre*, first staged by Filippo Taglioni for his daughter in St Petersburg, and revived for London in 1840. This lithograph by Bouvier records both the supernatural lightness of Taglioni's style and the idealisation of the ballerina by artists of the time. Poised on the very tip of her toe on a rose, Taglioni is here the personification of the ballerina as a spiritualised figure – in the ballet she was the ghost of a young girl who had died before she married the hero, and she is shown in the dream which was a large part of the ballet's action. The male dancer, despite his well-developed legs, is an accessory.

The subsidiary nature of the man's role in the Romantic Ballet can be appreciated in the four engravings shown here. They suggest the tremendous interest aroused by the ballet in the 1830s and 1840s, but each shows how the ballerina as heroine was manifesting herself as a vision of ideal beauty to the hero, and how the entire machinery of the ballet was structured towards this conception.

Left: In *La Sylphide* the sylph appears at the window as an intoxicating vision to James.

Above: In *Ondine* the beautiful sea sprite appears to Matteo.

Right: In *Le Délire d'un Peintre* we see Perrot as the painter who falls in love with a portrait (Fanny Elssler). *The Illustrated London News* commented that '*Le Délire* that she produces is not confined to the poor artist merely whom her beauty has captivated: all who look upon her become at once suddenly enthralled in a fascination like unto his; and whether she be in the picture frame or on the wings of her obedient volition as a flying muse, wonder and delight are equally called upon "to gaze and adore".' The ballerina was now supreme.

In 1843 Carlotta Grisi and Lucien Petipa came to London to repeat their triumphs of the previous year in *La Péri*, whose most celebrated moment was a leap in the sequence in which the Peri appeared to the hero during his opium dream. She dropped from a platform six feet above him into his arms. In his invaluable *The Romantic Ballet in Paris*, Ivor Guest records that 'The Parisian public soon showed itself to be very exacting with regard to the performance of the famous leap, in which Carlotta dropped gracefully, but like a stone, into Petipa's arms. Once, when she failed to perform it properly they made her repeat it three times before they would condescend to applaud her. Compare this with the reaction of a London audience, who begged her not to risk repeating it after a similar mis-timing at Drury Lane in the autumn, and gave her three hearty cheers when she fearlessly did it again. Not that the English were always so considerate: one of Queen Victoria's subjects was convinced that the ballet would eventually prove fatal to her, and did not miss a performance at the Opéra so that he might be present at her end.'

In passing we would note, though, that whatever the vicissitudes of the male dancer in the theatre, the social dance of the nineteenth century with its great dance crazes – for the Waltz and the Polka – and the great public balls which took place in Paris and London, showed no diminution of man's identity as the dominating figure in the social partnership. The man, it must be remembered, asked the woman to dance – a convention which has lasted in the ballroom almost until today.

Carlotta Grisi and James Silvain (né Sullivan) in *Paquita*. One of the most successful ballets of the Romantic age, *Paquita* was set in Spain during the Napoleonic wars. The military image presented by Silvain is very like that proposed by the music covers of the time for the quadrilles and polkas and waltzes that were so popular in the ballroom.

Above: The Polka as danced in New York in private houses in the 1840s. This music cover suggests the charm of domestic dancing which was so much a part of nineteenth-century family life.

Above: The Polka also had a tremendous vogue in the theatre, and the greatest stars of the Romantic age were seen in various versions of the dance, usually given a 'national' identity. Arthur St Léon and Fanny Cerrito danced a 'Lituana' polka, and they were invoked on the covers of piano sheet-music which was used to provide accompaniments to domestic dancing. The male dancer is portrayed at this time as an ardent, romantic swain.

Ballroom dancing received an injection of novelty with the arrival of folk dances adapted for social purposes. Interestingly, these dances maintained the same physical identity and dominance of the man – left: boisterous in the Polka (with its Bohemian ancestry); below: elegant in the Mazurka from Poland.

People have never stopped waltzing since the dance burst upon a shocked and astonished Europe at the turn of the nineteenth century. Left : The first extravagant and slightly lubricious association of the waltz is seen in a print showing dancers at the time of the Directoire – extravagant clothes and extravagant manners.
Below : In London the dance became refined and domesticated, as seen in this illustration from Thomas Wilson's *Manual of Waltzing* of 1817.

Left : A beautiful drawing by Gavarni shows the waltz at home in Paris in the 1840s.
Above : A rare photograph dated 1860 shows a ball in a Victorian house where demureness is all.

Top: Waltzers in Paris at the end of the nineteenth century in a ball given at the Hotel Sagan – this is the world of Proust's aristocracy. Above: The New York City Ballet in the final Rosenkavalier sequence from Balanchine's *Vienna Waltzes*. In this survey of 170 years of social dancing the man has remained the leading figure in the partnership and his dress, after the extravagances of the Directoire period, has remained constant.

It was in Russia, in the Imperial Ballet in St Petersburg, that ballet itself was preserved, and it was from here that the eventual revival of ballet as an art in the West, and with it the renewed validity of male dancing, was to come. The history of ballet in Russia during the nineteenth century is in effect a history of external influences absorbed into the mainstream of Russian ballet. A series of invited French ballet masters were to foster the development of ballet through teaching and choreography, culminating in the tremendous span of service given by Marius Petipa (1818–1910). Petipa arrived in Russia as a dancer in 1847. He served under two important French ballet masters, Jules Perrot and Arthur Saint Léon, before his assumption of the role of principal ballet master and choreographer in 1869 – a post he continued to hold until 1903. During this period Petipa produced that grand catalogue of full-length ballets which are the apogee of the nineteenth-century classic ballet. In such masterpieces as *La Bayadère*, *The Sleeping Beauty* and *Swan Lake* (which he choreographed with his assistant Lev Ivanov for the Petersburg ballet in 1895) Petipa brought to its glorious fruition the full-length spectacular ballet.

The central figure, the justification for these works, was however the ballerina, and Petipa's choreography can be seen as defining and enhancing the female dancer as a theatrical idol. Thanks to the participation of a series of guest ballerinas – most usually Italian – female virtuosity was superbly displayed in Petipa's work, and the gradual extension in the use of dancing on *pointe* (and the emergence of a stronger *pointe* shoe) meant that the range and nature of female virtuosity was much linked with dancing on toe.

But Petipa never could condone the debasement of the male dancer into the role of dim *porteur* – or, even worse, the girl *en travesti*. His ballets offered real dramatic range for the male dancer and the proper balance between the sexes was maintained in the working out of the ballet's story. Technically, men continued to be well trained in Russia, but they did not have many opportunities in Petipa's works to display their skills save in character roles and as princely figures. Nevertheless, male dancing was still respected in the classroom, and one of the important formative influences on dancing in Russia was Bournonville's schooling which was taken to Petersburg by his pupil the Swedish dancer Christian Johansson (1817–1903). Johansson went to Petersburg in 1841 and the rest of his career was effectively spent there, first as *premier danseur* and then as a hugely influential teacher. It was said by the Russian Nicholas Legat (1869–1937), himself a great dancer and teacher, that Petipa used to come to watch Johansson's classes, and when he left the room Johansson would observe, 'There's the old man picking up steps again', for it was acknowledged that Petipa was not as felicitous in writing male solos as he was in creating for the ballerina.

Nicholas Legat, and his younger brother Sergei, like their exemplar the noble first dancer Pavel Gerdt, upheld the traditions of the Russian *danseur*, but male dancing in Russia was to receive exceptional stimulus when Enrico Cecchetti, a Milanese virtuoso, appeared in Petersburg in 1887. A pupil of Giovanni Lepri, who was in turn a pupil of the great Italian pedagogue Carlo Blasis, Cecchetti – a tiny, bouncing figure – had prodigious technical skill and we can judge of his excellence from the role of the Blue

Bird in Petipa's *The Sleeping Beauty* which he created and which remains to this day a telling portrait of his brilliance.

By the beginning of the twentieth century, and the last years of Petipa's reign, a phenomenally gifted generation of dancers had been produced by the Petersburg school, both men and women. Ballet in Russia, though, had become so formalised, so trapped within the grand but marmoreal conventions of the Petipa style and the requirements of a hidebound aristocratic audience, that inevitably the young generation was eager for change. A first indication of this came with the aspirations of the Petersburg dancer Mikhail Fokine (1880–1942) to renew ballet by breaking away from the Petipa manner. He made his first innovations within the context of the Petersburg ballet, but his importance was only fully to be recognised when he became a creative voice in the early Russian seasons of opera and ballet presented by Serge Diaghilev in Paris.

Left: Mikhail Fokine as the hero in Petipa's one-act *La Halte de Cavalerie* (*The Cavalry Bivouac*) – the male dancer as charmer, *c.* 1900. At a time when the officers of the Imperial Russian Army were dressed with extraordinary glamour and opulence the stage image of the male dancer could exactly reflect this. There was no question about the virility of the danseur and no seeming inconsistency in showing him as a man of his time.

Above: Mikhail Mordkin in his *Bow and Arrow Dance*. Here is the Imperial Russian male dancer as ancient warrior – a strong image of a strong man.

Diaghilev (1872–1929) had begun his career in Russia as an organiser of art exhibitions and as a motive force behind the magazine *The World of Art*. By 1906 he had set about showing the riches of his native land to the West. An exhibition of Russian art in Paris in 1906 was followed in the next year by a series of concerts of Russian music, and in 1908 by an operatic season. Its success was such that in 1909 Diaghilev brought a combined operatic and balletic season, for which the dancers numbered the cream of the new young talents in Petersburg and Moscow – they included Pavlova, Karsavina and Nijinsky – shown in the choreographies of Fokine.

It was Fokine's staging of the Polovtsian Dances from *Prince Igor*, with the warrior horde led by the great actor-dancer Adolph Bolm, which caused a sensation at the opening of the Russian season of 1909. So did the soaring brilliance of the young Nijinsky, then only twenty-one years old, and these male virtuosos no less than the ballerinas were to announce the reawakening of public awareness of ballet as an art in the West. In 1910 Diaghilev returned with a group of dancers from Russia – this was the season which first saw *The Firebird* and *Scheherazade* – and in the following winter, when Nijinsky had been dismissed from the Imperial Ballet because his costuming at a performance of *Giselle* had allegedly offended the Dowager Empress, Diaghilev was confronted by the need to make a permanent troupe within which to show Nijinsky and to continue to present the new ballet of the twentieth century.

Nijinsky was a genius of the dance. It was truly said that when he put on the costume for a character he somehow magically became that character. And the exotic and mysterious roles which he performed – Petrushka, The Golden Slave in *Scheherazade*, the Poet in *Les Sylphides* and the Spirit of the Rose in *Le Spectre de la Rose* – mark the re-emergence of the male dancer as both star and interpretative artist. Diaghilev's own quest for novelty – guiding force in his entire career – led him to encourage Nijinsky to become a choreographer, and in *L'Après-midi d'un faune*, *Jeux*, and *Le Sacre du Printemps* a new image in choreography and dancing was to appear. *L'Après-midi*, the one ballet of Nijinsky's which survives in any comprehensible form, proposes walking as the basic idiom of the choreography, and its frankness in sexual matters suggests a new honesty in the depicting of a man on stage. The huge success of the Diaghilev seasons, particularly in Paris and London (the company was never seen in Russia), in the years before World War I marked the great awakening of Western taste for ballet. But it was a taste for 'Russian Ballet'; and there emerges at this time, and in the remaining years of the enterprise – which ended with Diaghilev's death in 1929 – the coincidental idea that the 'Russian' male dancer was the equal of the ballerina and in certain ballets even more important. This may be in part attributable to Diaghilev's homosexuality and his desire to shape the talents of the young male dancers whom he chose to turn into choreographers. Diaghilev broke with Nijinsky, his first great love in ballet, in 1913 when Nijinsky married. His next protégé was the young Moscow dancer Leonid Massine, whom he educated and encouraged, and whose dazzling intelligence was to make him the next choreographer to the Ballet Russe. Massine's dancing talent was essentially *demi-caractère* and dramatic, and his early ballets for Diaghilev – they include the masterly *Le Tricorne* and *La Boutique fantasque* of 1919 – are balletic dramas very different from anything that had gone before, and illuminated by fine male roles which Massine made for himself.

When, in 1921, Massine married the English dancer Vera Savina (Clark) he had to leave the Diaghilev entourage, though he was later to return to make further ballets for the company. Without a choreographer, Diaghilev decided to stage a magnificent revival of Petipa's *The Sleeping Beauty* (which Diaghilev retitled *The Sleeping Princess*, claiming that not all ballerinas were beauties.) It was produced in London in 1921, and was scheduled for a long run, though public indifference meant that it had to be withdrawn after 105 performances. Diaghilev recruited a magnificent assembly of ballerinas and soloists for the production, and in the matter of male dancing offered the contrasting talents of Pierre Vladimirov and Anatol Vilzak, who danced the Prince and were both formerly first dancers in St Petersburg (and later very influential teachers in America). The role of the Blue Bird was most closely associated with Stanislas Idzikowski, a dazzling virtuoso and a pupil of Maestro Cecchetti. Thirty years before, Cecchetti had created the role of the Blue Bird which was a tribute to his technical brilliance from Marius Petipa, the choreographer. A second tribute had been the fact that the role of the fairy Carabosse was also made for Cecchetti, to show off his skill as a mime. Now, in 1921, as teacher to the Diaghilev company, Cecchetti returned to the stage for a single performance to the role of Carabosse.

The staging also involved a young Anglo-Irish dancer who was to take the stage name Anton Dolin. This was the beginning of a remarkable career. Dolin was to reach public acclaim first in ballets by Diaghilev's next choreographer, Bronislava Nijinska (Nijinsky's sister), and in *Le Train bleu* the new sporting image of the male dancer which Nijinska had already announced in her earlier ballet *Les Biches* – with its three athletes from the beach intruding into a house party – was further developed. Dolin's acrobatic skill inspired Jean Cocteau, author of the ballet's libretto, to conceive a role for a beautiful young playboy – Le Beau Gosse (the Handsome Kid) – who performed handstands and various other 'stunts'.

Inspired by the sporting pleasures of life in the South of France (like *Les Biches*, which had a similar setting) the male dancer was entirely liberated from the traditional image of the man as 'ballet dancer'. Diaghilev's affection for, and obsession with, youth, and the arrival of Serge Lifar into his life in 1924 as his protégé, brought a series of works which glorified the young man as hero. In *Zéphyr et Flore*, in *Barabau*, *Roméo et Juliette* (in which Lifar as a twenty-year-old Romeo wore aviator's gear to elope with Karsavina, then in her 40s, as Juliet), in *La Pastorale* in which Lifar was an errand boy, in *La Chatte* in which he was brought on, heroic in the arms of a group of male companions, and, supremely, in *Apollo* and *The Prodigal Son*, Lifar's beauty and physical allure provided a further impulse for public admiration of the young male as star. Diaghilev had other fine male dancers, notably the Pole Leon Woizikowski, an amazing and virile character dancer; during the late 1920s Anton Dolin, Idzikowski and Massine all returned to dance for him. Until Diaghilev's death in 1929 his male dancers were of equal importance to the females and of prime significance in the creative life of his company.

Anton Dolin and Leon Woizikowski in *Le Train bleu* of 1924, staged by Diaghilev's Ballet Russe. The ballet was inspired by Dolin's athletic skill and it affords an interesting contrast with the innovation of *Jeux* just eleven years before, the first ballet to show sporting types on stage. Dolin and Woizikowski and the whole cast were dressed by Chanel.

It is the 1930s – a time when national ballets were gradually establishing themselves in Britain and the United States – that reinforced the public view that only acceptable male dancers were Russian or at least Russian-named. There emerged in 1932 a reborn Russian Ballet, based in Monte Carlo and moulded very much in the image of the Diaghilev enterprise. At first its claim to public attention was the presence of three prodigiously gifted adolescent girls, Tatiana Riabouchinska, Tamara Toumanova and Irina Baronova, dubbed the 'baby ballerinas', who were to inspire Balanchine and Massine to create ballets for them. Balanchine had joined Diaghilev from Petrograd in 1924, and had been the final ballet master to the Diaghilev company, where he had early proved his genius as choreographer. He next accepted an invitation to go to the United States, and from 1934 he and Lincoln Kirstein, his patron and artistic associate, were to set about creating the American classic ballet.

It was Leonid Massine who became the creative force within the Ballet Russe. His ballets dominated the repertory of the company that had been set up after Diaghilev's death by René Blum and Colonel de Basil, and then from 1938 of a second troupe which was formed as a rival to de Basil and of which Massine was artistic director and again motive force. In both of these Ballet Russe troupes the male dancer was still an important figure, and the generation of *danseurs* who now emerged could boast such magnificent talents as Yurek Shabelevsky, David Lichine, André Eglevsky, Igor Youskevitch, Frederic Franklin, Roman Jasinsky in addition, of course, to Massine himself, Woizikowski, and Dolin, with the occasional appearances also of Serge Lifar. Lifar's greater contribution, though, came as choreographer and principal male star of the ballet at the Paris Opéra, where for nearly thirty years he produced a considerable list of ballets in many of which his own talents as interpreter were justification for the action: *Icare*, *David Triomphant*, *Alexandre Le Grand*, *Le Chevalier et la Damoiselle*, and *Joan de Zarissa*, among others, were major works which placed the male dancer firmly in the centre of the stage.

The 'Russianness' of the Ballet Russe of the 1930s was in essence false. The male dancers were mostly the pupils of émigré teachers who had fled Russia at the time of the Revolution. The characters they represented on stage were exotic or poetic, or abstract figures shown off in the series of ballets set to symphonies that Massine now produced. Whatever the excellence of their technique and the excitement of their stage presence, they were essentially 'foreign' to the world of their time. In fact, like the Ballet Russe companies, they were a doomed breed. The rootless and gypsy life of the touring Ballet Russe was to prove fatal to the companies' artistic existence. With neither home nor school, they existed on the dedication and almost claustrophobic intensity of their identity as touring ensembles. The Ballet Russe companies were massively popular during the 1930s and reached a huge audience. They were instrumental not only in holding the public's interest in ballet during the years after the death of Diaghilev but also in widening it: it was entirely due to the 'Russian Ballet' that new audiences were won throughout the United States of America and also in Australia.

But more significant in the long run were the moves made during the 1930s to

establish truly national companies in Britain and the United States. The work of Marie Rambert and especially of Ninette de Valois in Britain, and of George Balanchine and Lincoln Kirstein in the United States, was in direct contrast to the glamour and brief seasons of the émigré Russians. Working without any state support, and reliant upon the products of their schools, these national ballets were, in the matter of male dancing, faced with many problems. These combined the dreadful shortage of funds with appalling prejudice against ballet as a career for a boy and the belief fostered by the Ballet Russe that it was a Russian art. (In the series of hilarious novels in which Caryl Brahms and S. J. Simon celebrated the popularity of the Russian Ballet in the 1930s there is the alarming figure of the renamed *danseur* Ernest Smithsky – who was no Nijinsky.)

Public mistrust of male dancers, and the belief that ballet shoes were a sign of rampant effeminacy, was, alas, clearly to be seen in revue sketches: the mincing male dancer was always good for a laugh. It took many years for this view even to start to disappear. That most male dancers were called up for military service during World War II meant that war-time repertories were inevitably geared towards ballets in which the male role was secondary. An outstanding exception in Britain, though, was Robert Helpmann, an Australian who achieved huge popular success in his first appearances with the Vic-Wells Ballet and who sustained the creative life of the company, by then the Sadler's Wells (now Royal) Ballet during the war with his ballets, *Comus, Hamlet, Miracle in the Gorbals*, all of which contained star roles for his own vivid dramatic talents.

Left: Kurt Jooss (1901–79), the German dancer and choreographer, was a pupil of the theoretician Rudolf von Laban. He came to international attention when his dance work *The Green Table* won a choreographic competition in 1932 in Paris. It encouraged Jooss to form his own company, the Ballets Jooss, which survived in various incarnations for twenty years. Jooss's choreographies relied upon strong male dancing and *The Green Table*, which is his most famous work, was dominated by the figure of Death (created by Jooss himself) with three strong secondary roles, the Profiteer, the Standard Bearer and the young Soldier. Dealing with the futility of war, *The Green Table* has remained in several repertories today. Our illustration shows Hans Zullig, one of Jooss's finest artists (right), as the young Soldier taking leave of the young girl, as the Standard Bearer summons him to war.

Harald Kreutzberg (1902–1968) was the foremost male dancer in the Central European style. A pupil of Mary Wigman, his dancing asserted the validity of the male image at a time when much Central European dancing was dominated by women.

It was the Lifar tradition which was to be responsible for that excellence of French male dancing which continues to this day. A fundamental is the quality of instruction at the Paris Opéra School and in the immediately postwar years French male dancers in various companies ranked in importance and public esteem with the ballerinas. These years also saw a remarkable explosion of ballet activity surrounding Roland Petit, who trained at the Paris Opéra but at the age of twenty was to be instrumental in the foundation of Les Ballets des Champs Elysées. This company, which enjoyed a brief but glorious span of creativity, showed Petit himself as a superb dance actor (a quality which he retains to this day) but its chief revelation was the dancing of Jean Babilée. Born in 1923, educated in the Opéra School, he had both a dazzling classical technique and a magnetic stage presence. Undoubtedly one of the greatest dancers of this century, Babilée could take away the breath of an audience by the superb elevation and clarity of his dancing in the Blue Bird *pas de deux*, and exert an absolute control over the public's emotions as the young suicide in Petit's *Le Jeune Homme et la Mort* or as the hunchback in Petit's *Le Rendez-vous* or as the Joker in Janine Charrat's *Jeu de Cartes*. A dancer of genius, he has latterly been seen in *Life*, a specially created study for him by Maurice Béjart.

These two photographs offer contrasting views of Jean Babilée, the greatest dancer of his generation, both as virtuoso and as dramatic performer. He is seen right as the Blue Bird in Petipa's *Sleeping Beauty*, a role in which he touched perfection, and below he is seen in a contemporary role in his own ballet, *La Boucle*, staged in 1957. It was part of Babilée's genius to seem equally at home in fantasy roles and also as intensely modern figures, such as the suicidal young man in *Le Jeune Homme et la Mort* or the hunchback in *Le Rendez-vous*, both roles created for him by Roland Petit.

Left: *Le Jeune Homme et la Mort* created a sensation when it was first performed. The ballet was inspired by Jean Cocteau and told of a young man in a Parisian garret awaiting his girl friend. When the girl arrives she is revealed to be Death. After an extraordinary battle, both physical and temperamental, which is shown in this photograph, the girl leaves and the young man commits suicide by hanging himself and a final scene reveals the girl as Death walking over the roofs of Paris towards him. Babilée's acrobatic skills were tremendously explored by Roland Petit's choreography – he was the incarnation of existential youth of immediately post-war France.

Top left: Richard Cragun rehearsing the role of Quasimodo, the tragic hunchback, in Roland Petit's *Notre Dame de Paris* with the Ballet National de Marseille. Bottom left and above: Jean Guizerix of the Paris Opéra Ballet in rehearsal. Guizerix, one of the leading stars of the Opéra is a dancer who combines extraordinary technical power with intensity of dramatic presence; he is one of the greatest dancers of our time.

Contemporary with Petit and Babilée were such exceptional artists as Vladimir Skouratoff, a poetic *premier danseur classique*, the mercurial Serge Golovine and the noble Youly Algaroff, artists who appeared with the cosmopolitan Grand Ballet du Marquis de Cuevas. The Paris Opéra itself had no shortage of fine male dancing, and performances by Michel Renault and Alexandre Kalioujny in the 1940s and 1950s asserted the importance of male artistry at the Opéra. The tradition continues today: witness the power and intensity of Jean Guizerix and the elegance of Michael Denard, while the younger leaders of the company include the exceptional Charles Jude and Patrick Dupond, already idolised by a huge public.

In one other company, adored in France and Italy as well as in its native Belgium, and created and inspired by the French-born Maurice Béjart, the importance of the male dancer is today strongly proclaimed. Le Ballet du XXème Siècle, based in Brussels, and, during the last two decades, a phenomenon of the ballet world in its immense popular success, has always shown a marvellous male ensemble and Maurice Béjart has reasserted the importance of the male dancer in many of his ballet spectacles. In *Golestan*, a Persian extravaganza, an entry for male dancers seems like a masculine equivalent of the entry of the Shades in *La Bayadère*, while such diverse pieces as *Nijinsky, Clown of God, Songs of a Wayfarer* and *Notre Faust* are among many works which give the centre of the stage to the male dancer. (Béjart's *Boléro*, to the Ravel score, was first seen in 1961 and featured a ballerina dancing on an immense table surrounded by a couple of dozen palpitating male admirers. Later the sexual roles were reversed and a male dancer was the focus of the admiration of a cohort of women. Most recently an all-male version has been revealed.)

The appearance of the male corps de ballet in Maurice Béjart's *Golestan* for the Ballet du XXème Siècle.

The sum effect of Béjart's choreography for men, though, seems less concerned with the male as dancer than with the male as body beautiful to be admired. (Béjart has declared 'dance is a man's affair'.) There is an element of display of masculine physique as opposed to masculine technique which is almost narcissistic. For a more cogent view of the male dancer we find that George Balanchine's choreography, despite his statement 'ballet is woman', presents a clean and uncompromisingly virile image of the male dancer as a man who dances and also expresses man's quest for a woman as partner and inspiration. A recurrent theme of Balanchine's choreographies is this portrait of man idolising and idealising the female, which was also the function of Balanchine's choreographic creativity: works as diverse as *Night Shadow*, *Duo Concertant*, and *Robert Schumann's Davidsbündlertänze* suffice as examples.

Igor Youskevitch in Balanchine's *Theme and Variations* with American Ballet Theatre at Covent Garden in 1950. This action photograph shows the great danseur noble in the sensational entry which he made in the man's variation in this magnificent ballet.

In other forms of theatre – in the musical, in the music hall and in the cinema – during the 1930s, male dancing had never gone into eclipse. The traditions of dancing as a popular theatrical entertainment meant that eccentric dancing and tap dancing, and the explosive energies of black American dancing, were never questioned as superb entertainment. The male dancer in the social setting was entirely respected, and the emergence of the distinguished ballroom exhibition dancers Vernon and Irene Castle was a prelude to the great and continuing popularity of social dancing, not only as a recreation but also as an entertainment. In the theatre such elegant performers as Fred and Adele Astaire and Jack Buchanan became public idols. The image of the 'top hat and tails' male dancer was to become one of the central facts in the magnificence of Fred Astaire's work in the cinema. Often, and rightly, called the greatest dancer of the century, Astaire was also one of the greatest stars in Hollywood, and he succeeded in creating an image of peerless ease and extreme brilliance which was to condition public response to male dancing anywhere but in the ballet theatre.

Since the heyday of Astaire's cinema career as a dancer, the popularity of male dancing on film has never waned. Films like *Seven Brides for Seven Brothers*, Gene Kelly's dance films, and the most recent success of John Travolta, have confirmed public taste for the dancing man with whom they can readily identify. In a sense the cinema here fulfils its function as a mirror to the life which its audience lives. This can never be said to be true on superficial terms of the ballet theatre. The remoteness of image in the roles taken by male dancers, and the sophistication and alien form of their dance language, mean that public response to a *danseur* has to overcome a barrier which never separated the dancing styles of the cinema from its audience. Without aspiring to be an Astaire, any reasonably agile man could see himself as a tap dancer, while the later energies of the Disco speak a language for everyone to understand and enjoy. It is inconceivable, though, that a man would be able to emulate a male ballet dancer. Unless years of training have been received during adolesence the simplest ballet steps are impossible.

Some indication of changing attitudes towards the male dancer, and of the power of television to educate an audience, came with an innovatory television programme shown in December 1959 in the United States. With the positive title *Dancing is a Man's Game* it brought Gene Kelly as presenter and polemicist to tell 'TV audiences that dancing isn't "sissy stuff"'. Reviewing the programme in *Dance Magazine* Ann Barzel, the distinguished dance commentator and critic, said: 'Millions of viewers could not help but be affected by its message . . . "Dancing is a man's game." announced Kelly as he climbed down a ladder into a busy gymn, where Mickey Mantle slid for a base, Sugar Ray Robinson hit a bag, Vic Seixas lobbed tennis balls, Bob Cousey bounced a basket ball, and other champion athletes made movements familiar to their fans. Five men in tights went through the cleancut exercises of classic ballet. Eventually they took the competitive movements of the athletes, abstracted them and distilled them into economical, straightforward, beautiful movements of dance. These were uncontroversially virile. No one had to point it out. And you were acutely conscious of how much more satisfying they were when done by the finer muscled, better postured dancers.

Right: Fred Astaire and Ginger Rogers in *Swing Time*, 1934, and below, Fred Astaire in *Three Little Words*, 1950. It would be impossible to overestimate the importance of Fred Astaire or the significance of the image he presented of the male dancer. Always elegant, disguising prodigious gifts under a relaxed and charming air, he is one of the great geniuses of the dance, and the cinema has happily made his genius immortal.

Right: Vernon and Irene Castle dancing the Maxixe. The Castles in the immediate pre-First World War years epitomised the elegance and refinement possible in exhibitions of social dancing. They set standards in dress and behaviour which were widely emulated. Vernon Castle was killed on active service in the First World War.

Eleanor Powell and Fred Astaire, a shining black floor and leggy chorines, in *Broadway Melody of 1940*. The scene is oddly reminiscent of *Les Sylphides*, with Astaire as the sole man amid a bevy of idealised womanhood.

Below : John Travolta in *Staying Alive*. In this and his previous film *Saturday Night Fever* the male dancer is identified as a new hero.

'Edward Villella of New York City Ballet demonstrated the virtuosity of the male dancer in an *enchaînement* of double beats and pirouettes. It was magnificent. A little later on in the programme he made a tremendous, almost superhuman contribution. To show the athleticism of dance and the grace of ice skating, he was presented along with champion figure skater Dick Button. They alternated in parallel tricks involving jumping and turning, and finished together in a competitive finale on a split screen. It proved that ice skating was as graceful as dancing, but it also subjected Villella to a competition as gruelling as those of mythology, in which heroes were pitted against gods. Or it was like the races of horse versus steam engine. For Eddie Villella in ballet slippers, with only his trained muscles and stout heart, was a brilliant match for a man aided by the superhuman speed and bounce produced by steel blades on slick ice.'

We have to admit that male dancing in ballet in the West was a struggling plant during the period just before and after the Second World War. The box office glamour of the Ballet Russe was fading, and the emergent national companies had still to make their mark on the larger public and win an audience capable of sustaining their development. Public prejudice and financial insecurity were the twin hazards to the male dancer's career. It was the pioneer work of the national ballet schools – like the Royal Ballet School and the School of American Ballet – which eventually recruited boys from the age of eleven and were able to give them that serious training and proper status which were to provide hope for the future. The emergence of fine young dancers in the late 1940s and 1950s – such artists as the late David Blair of the Royal Ballet, and Jacques d'Amboise of the New York City Ballet, whose masculinity and great physical charm were a fresh image for the *danseur* in the West – set a pattern which has brought the standard of male dancing to its present high point throughout the world. A central figure in the new public acclamation for the male dancer has been Rudolf Nureyev, and it is impossible to overestimate his importance.

Of Tartar descent, he came to dancing late, but his determination – and the ample opportunities offered to the male dancer in Soviet Russia – meant that he was able to attend the ballet school in Leningrad from the age of seventeen, where he was a pupil of the celebrated teacher Alexander Pushkin. He was early on marked for greatness in the Kirov Ballet, but in 1961, on the occasion of the Kirov's first visit to Paris, he chose to seek asylum in the West and there began that career as an international star which has made him the best-known name in the ballet of our time. A prodigious temperament, a great gift for dancing, and an unquenchable appetite for hard work, allied to his charismatic personality, have meant that he has been able to dance anywhere and fill a theatre. The 'man in the street' (and the 'woman in the street') may not know much about ballet, but they know that the name Nureyev is synonymous with theatrical excitement. Like Nijinsky, or Pavlova – or Maria Callas – he has crossed every barrier of taste and become a universal symbol.

Nureyev's appearance on the ballet stage coincided with a great expansion in male dancing which he both led and symbolised. The social attitudes of the 1960s, with their greater freedoms, meant that many young men who might have previously considered

By the time she came to make *Night Journey* in 1947, Martha Graham had recruited several fine male dancers to her troupe. *Night Journey* was a version of the Oedipus myth, and our illustration shows Graham as Jocasta ensnared, with Bertram Ross as Oedipus. Behind them, Robert Cohan is the blind seer Tiresias. Ross's heroic physique inspired several important roles, among them *Seraphic Dialogue*, and *Embattled Garden*. Cohan was to become the vital influence which made possible the establishing of Graham technique in Britain.

the idea of dancing and rejected it, were now able to look again at their aspiration and decide to make it come true. This was due to increased opportunities for study and to a very great popularity for dance, both balletic and contemporary.

'Modern dance' or 'contemporary dance' was a theatrical art which had emerged in the early years of this century thanks to the innovative work of such female dancers as Isadora Duncan and Ruth St Denis. Its early and formative years were much dominated by women: Mary Wigman in Germany, Doris Humphrey and Martha Graham in the United States, were among its great exponents.

It is understandable that in America during the 1920s and 1930s the idea of a young man taking up modern dance was quite as preposterous as the idea of his taking up ballet. Nevertheless, a few pioneer figures did emerge. Ruth St Denis was joined by Ted Shawn, a would-be Baptist minister who had taken up dancing. He became her partner initially in social dance displays and later, with their own Denishawn company, in highly theatrical and often exotic entertainments. When their partnership broke up Shawn struck a blow for male dancing by forming his troupe of 'Men Dancers' who performed successfully throughout the United States. In the years between 1933 and 1939 it was Shawn's aim to re-establish, as the American critic Walter Terry put it, 'the right of men to dance'.

Ruth St Denis and Ted Shawn in *Ourieda – a Romance of the Desert*, one of their exotic numbers which they first danced in 1914, the year of their marriage. In dances like this, with their vivid local colour, they were able to titillate the appetite of their audience.

But it was not until after World War II that there came the upsurge of young men's interest in dancing in America. This was in part due to the lately established presence of modern dance in the curricula of American colleges, and also to the public's increasing awareness of the work of Martha Graham and her contemporaries, including Charles Weidman, Erick Hawkins and José Limón. Thus we find such influential dancers and creators as Merce Cunningham, Paul Taylor and Robert Cohan starting their careers as dancers with Graham and then leaving – in the process of secession traditional in contemporary dance – to found their own companies and choreographic styles.

In their wake have come generations of young men who no longer find it difficult to take up dancing as a career and are no longer considered as in some way 'special' or

Ted Shawn and his Men Dancers in *Olympiad*, one of the typically athletic creations made by Shawn for his male company during the 1930s. Here, for a new audience, was an immediately identifiable image of the male dancer as athlete.

'unusual'. Robert Cohan's influence has been especially strong in Britain, in that he was invited in 1967 to found a school in London to teach authentic Graham technique, and from his school there eventually emerged today's London Contemporary Dance Theatre. By the example of its admirable technical training and by its willingness to take dance into schools and communities, colleges and regional theatres, LCDT has opened up new vistas of dancing for a new audience and has inspired many young men to see dancing as an exciting and rewarding theatrical career. The result is a company of wonderful technical accomplishment in which the work of its men is of outstanding impact. LCDT's Patrick Harding-Irmer, his colleagues Darshan Bhuller and Michael Small, are fine advocates of the exhilaration and integrity of male dancing today.

Erick Hawkins was born in 1909 and studied both at the School of American Ballet and with Harald Kreutzberg. This breadth of training was reflected in his career, for he danced with Balanchine's prewar companies and then joined Martha Graham in 1938 as her first major male dancer (and husband). In 1951 he formed his own company, for which he has made many ballets, including *Geography of Noon*, in which he is seen here.

José Limón (1908–72) in his own *Danzas Mexicanas*. Limón began his career with the Humphrey-Weidman troupe and was a principal dancer in the company for ten years, creating many leading roles and also providing choreography for the company. In 1939 he staged his suite of Mexican dances, finding in his national heritage (he was born in Culiacán, Mexico) inspiration for dance portraits which made great use of the expressive power and physical boldness which marked his dancing.

However doubtful the identity of the male dancer in the western dance theatre in this century, the male dancer has never been a subject for ridicule in Russia. Building on the achievements of the old Imperial Russian Ballet, Soviet ballet confirmed the importance of man in ballet in a new society. The strong traditions of folk dance throughout Russia have always recognised the muscular bravura and virility of male dancing. As Soviet ballet emerged as a definite art form in the 1920s and 1930s, the Russian male dancer remained a figure of considerable importance.

This was in no small part due to the themes: the first truly successful Soviet ballet, *The Red Poppy* of 1927, made great show of male dancing both in the sailors' dance and in two extraordinary solos devised for the celebrated virtuoso, Asaf Messerer. *The Red Poppy*, which told of the support offered by a Soviet ship to oppressed Chinese workers, indicated something of the 'heroic' identity which was to be assumed by the male dancer. In the ballets which followed in its wake, the elements of struggle to overcome oppression, the use of politically-acceptable subjects, stressed the identity of the male dancer as a very 'positive' and dominant force. So, works like *The Flames of Paris*, which dealt with the French Revolution, or *Laurencia*, which was based on a Spanish tragedy, or in narratives taken from Russian history and Russian and world literature, the power of the Russian male dancer and, in turn, the image of male dancing were strengthened and made more valiant and daring.

Talking about two of the great stars of Soviet Ballet, the Russian author George Mamontov said of Alexei Yermolayev, who made his debut in 1925: 'Yermolayev's dance gradually assumed new outlines, dictated by the new substance of ballet performances in tune with contemporary Soviet life. Yermolayev perceived the necessity of making the male dance heroic, and he gained a firm footing for the male hero in the Soviet ballet.' Of the other, Vakhtang Chabukiany, who graduated in 1928, Mamontov wrote that his dance 'calls to action, braces for action and is in itself a hymn to struggle'.

With these two examples and that of Asaf Messerer, and with the continuing and contrasted tradition of the classical *danseur noble* personified by the Leningrad *premier danseur* Konstantin Sergeyev, it is small wonder that the variety and richness of Soviet male dancing has been an impressive component in its theatrical success. It is no exaggeration to talk of the revelation of Russian male dancing which came with the first appearances in the West of the Bolshoi Ballet in 1956, and of the Kirov Ballet in 1961, as being comparable to the revelation of the first Diaghilev seasons.

Such Bolshoi artists as Yuri Zhdanov and Nicolai Fadeyechev, Georgi Farmanyantz, Gleb Yevdokimov and Alexander Lapauri, and the Kirov stars Yuri Soloviev, Oleg Sokolov and Vladilen Semenov, showed entirely new horizons in male dancing. Their successors today, the Bolshoi's Vladimir Vasiliev and Vyacheslav Gordeyev, sustain this image of male excellence, and the repertory in Moscow particularly does much to promote the blazing image of the male dancer. Yuri Grigorovich, director and chief choreographer of the Bolshoi Ballet, has drawn astounding portraits of men dancing in his *Spartacus* and *Ivan the Terrible*. In these ballets we see the powerful surge of energy and the tireless virtuosity that is the hallmark of Moscow bravura.

The nineteenth-century classical ballets surviving in the Soviet repertory provided an example for later creativity. In Leningrad the male dancer continued the elegant traditions of the old Imperial Ballet, seen above left, where Konstantin Sergeyev is Siegfried and Galina Ulanova Odette in the 1939 staging of *Swan Lake*. His costume is that obligatory for princely figures. In the Soviet ballet *The Flames of Paris*, first performed in Leningrad in 1932 with choreography by Vainonen, the male image was more democratic as we see above right, with the great Georgian dancer Vakhtang Chabukiany partnering Muza Gottlieb.

The Kirov Ballet has inevitably suffered from the loss of two of the greatest dancers of the century. We have already considered the importance of Rudolf Nureyev; in Mikhail Baryshnikov the Soviet ballet training system at its most elegant in Leningrad found superlative material which it shaped into a unique classic artist. Baryshnikov was a pupil of the great Alexander Pushkin in the Kirov School, and he entered the Kirov Ballet in 1967. By then he had won a gold medal at the Varna Ballet Competition of 1966, following this with a gold medal at the Moscow Ballet Competition of 1969. His appearance in London in 1970 was a revelation of classic perfection in style and manner (in this he resembled his colleague, the superlative Yuri Soloviev who died tragically in 1977). But the artistic constraints of Soviet Ballet impelled Baryshnikov, as they had impelled Nureyev and Natalia Makarova, to defect to the West. Since 1974 Baryshnikov has made an immense impact on Western ballet, as a virtuoso and as a dance-actor of exceptional expressive power, as the star of a dance film, *The Turning Point*, and in television spectaculars. It is some comment on this public impact that in May 1975 he was featured on the front cover of both *Time Magazine* and *Newsweek*. His western career has been international, but it has been based upon American Ballet Theatre, of which company he became director in 1980.

Rudolf Nureyev has similarly become director of a ballet company, that of the Paris Opéra, and in the twenty-two years of his western career he has unquestionably danced more performances with more companies and in more ballets than any other male dancer in history. His energy, like his eagerness for work, has been an amazement and a delight to his audiences and he thinks nothing of embarking upon five-week seasons in which companies succeed each other as his framework, while the advertisements proclaim 'Rudolf Nureyev will dance at every performance'.

The success and great talent of Nureyev and of Baryshnikov have been both example and inspiration for the developing interest in male dancing in the West. This has been seen with the Royal Ballet's Anthony Dowell and David Wall, and Fernando Bujones of American Ballet Theatre and with Jorge Donn of Maurice Béjart's Ballet du XXème Siècle. Everywhere now the male dancer is presented as the equal of the ballerina in artistic as well as public importance, and choreographers today are, more than ever before, concerned with exploring the full range of male dancing and acting. Many of

At the end of the first act of *The Fountain of Bakhchisaray*, a ballet based on Pushkin's poem, choreographed by Zakharov and staged in Leningrad in 1934, Tartar hordes attack and burn a Polish manor house. This scene has been one of the great showpieces of Soviet ballet both for its stage effects – the house goes up in flames – and for the power of the male dancing.

the works of Maurice Béjart with the Ballet du XXème Siècle in Brussels, or of John Neumeier with the Hamburg Ballet, have extended the range and significance of male dancing. Even in the New York City Ballet, dedicated to George Balanchine's dictum that 'ballet is woman', the predominantly female repertory has yielded to the presence of such fine male stars as Peter Martins, Helgi Tomasson, Ib Andersen and Sean Lavery.

In Britain Anthony Dowell brought the English classic style to world attention through the elegance and purity of his performances with the Royal Ballet. To David Wall, a highly gifted dance-actor, came the distinction of creating one of the most arduous roles ever written for a man, that of the Archduke Rudolf in Kenneth MacMillan's sensational *Mayerling*, whose three acts charted the terrifying moral decline of the heir to the Austro-Hungarian throne. In popularising dance with a more general audience one other Royal Ballet artist has been notably significant: Wayne Sleep, a virtuoso dancer and born entertainer, has reached a new audience through his appearances on television and in musicals.

The folk dance ensemble directed by Igor Moiseyev made a tremendous impact in the West on its tours during the 1950s. Devoted at that time to the richness of Soviet folk dance, it also contained such specially choreographed showpieces as the hilarious *Football*, in which the audience was entirely convinced that a particularly boisterous game was in progress – although there was no actual ball.

There is one European nation in which the male dancer in the theatre has maintained an unchangingly important and virile image. This is Denmark, where the Royal Danish Ballet has preserved the attitudes to dancing which were first proposed by Auguste Bournonville. It was Bournonville, a fine dancer and a pupil of Auguste Vestris, who assumed directorship of the moribund ballet in Copenhagen in 1830 and brought it to full and magnificent life. For forty-seven years he directed its fortunes, creating vivid and beautiful choreography and transmitting his French ballet training to generations of dancers. Because he was himself a talented dancer, he saw no reason why his ballets need reflect the Romantic era's decline of the *danseur* as a significant figure in choreography. Thus, in his ballets, he was always at pains to preserve the correct balance between the sexes, and he could well justify some of his early ballets on the importance of the man's role rather than that of the ballerina. He established a tradition of technical brilliance and dramatic urgency for the male dancer which is still maintained in Denmark.

Bournonville, loving his career and believing it to be the finest in the world, was also determined that female dancers should not be the socially-suspect figures that they were elsewhere. His insistence upon the moral decency of his female dancers, and the highly honourable portraits of women which his ballets drew, contributed to reasserting the respectability of women on and off the ballet stage as companions to his virile and morally-upright male characters. In practical terms the Bournonville tradition in Copenhagen has meant that male dancing has always been of exceptional importance there, and Danish training for men is still superior than that for women.

The strength of Danish male dancing – its lightness and bounding grace – has served as a touchstone for male dancers everywhere. It was no accident that Christian Johannsson, Bournonville's pupil, became a great dancer and vital teacher in Imperial Petersburg for over sixty years, and it is no accident that today the New York City Ballet and the School of American Ballet should call upon Danish dancers and Danish teaching to guarantee excellence of male training.

Although – as everywhere in Europe – the Danish Ballet knew its fallow periods, the distinction of its teaching has guaranteed a constant flow of superb male dancers. Some have remained at home and their careers have been spent in the service of the Royal Danish Ballet whose masculine repertory encompasses both dazzling virtuosity and intense dramatic expression (the Danish balletic mime tradition is unrivalled anywhere in the world). There is, additionally, a continuity of service and performance in Denmark which means that when male virtuosos reach that age when technical brilliance is fading, there yet remains a grand repository of dramatic and comic roles in which their artistry can continue to develop. In Denmark the character and mime roles are thought no less important than the most taxing dance assignments; indeed, without the dramatic setting in Bournonville's works, the dance divertissements could not shine so brightly. So, an outstanding *danseur* like Fredbjørn Bjørnsson has moved on from the bravura roles of his early career to assume character roles in which he is no less exciting. Similarly Niels Kehlet, an artist of greatness, was seen during the 1979 Bournonville festival both as the soaring hero of *Napoli* and as the comic bumpkin Geert in *Kermesse in Bruges*.

Peter Schaufuss in *Etudes* with London Festival Ballet. Harald Lander's *Etudes* is one of those ballets which celebrate the excitements of ballet training by showing the gradual progression from simple exercises at the barre to the most dazzling feats of virtuosity. First staged for the Royal Danish Ballet in 1948, it has since entered many repertories and the Danish-trained Schaufuss brings to it all the bravura and classic elegance that the principal male role requires.

It has been the tradition of the Royal Danish Ballet since 1946 that its *danseurs* should appear as ambassadors of the Bournonville School with many companies, making exceptional careers away from their native land. The first such case was that of Erik Bruhn, a classical dancer of unrivalled nobility and elegance, who astounded a wider public by the purity and virtuosity of his dancing. (Bruhn was a pupil of Hans Beck, who was himself a pupil of Bournonville, who was a pupil of Vestris. Such clear artistic lineage is in itself of obvious value.) His unique quality was admired not only in the West but caused a sensation in Russia when he danced there with American Ballet Theatre in 1960.

In New York the New York City Ballet has acknowledged the value of Danish training by engaging the notable Danish teacher Stanley Williams to take an active part in instruction in its school, while offering a home for Peter Martins (now one of the company's two chief ballet masters), Ib Andersen and Adam Lüders, all products of the Royal Danish Ballet School.

Peter Schaufuss, son of two celebrated artists of the Royal Danish Ballet, Frank Schaufuss and the late Mona Vangsaae, graduated into the Royal Danish Ballet from its school, but soon spread his wings in the by-now-traditional fashion. Through his appearances with the National Ballet of Canada, London Festival Ballet, the Paris Opéra Ballet, the New York City Ballet, the Berlin Ballet, and latterly with the Royal Ballet, Schaufuss has gained a large international following for his grand virtuosity. He has also proved a most eloquent advocate for Bournonville choreographies as well as Bournonville training, in skilled stagings of *La Sylphide*, *Napoli* and *A Folk Tale* which have revealed his ability to give these masterworks continued life in the repertories of companies outside Denmark.

The career of Peter Schaufuss, like that of the other great dancers we have mentioned in today's dance theatre, underlines the fact that dancing in all its aspects is now once again a man's game. There might seem no obvious link between the stardom of John Travolta and of Mikhail Baryshnikov, or between the excitement generated by John Curry on ice and Patrick Dupond at the Paris Opéra, but they all assert the vitality and brilliance of the male dancer. The athleticism implicit in their work is powerful – as it is in such wild dance activities as 'Breaking' and 'Slamming' – and it tells of the present status of the dancing man as hero, no matter what his dance style.

Right: Darshan Bhuller of the London Contemporary Dance Theatre.

To Control the Attack: the Dancer as Athlete

Male dancing borders on athleticism and borders on poetic qualities. That's the main challenge – to have that marvellous virility and at the same time to be a beautiful man and move in a beautiful manner. Masculinity in dance is a fantastic attack and at the same time a delicate restraint. The difficulty is to control the attack.

Edward Villella, *Dance Perspectives No. 40*

Martha Graham called one of her dance works *Acrobats of God*, a reference to the theological comment that certain early Christian fathers were *athletae Dei*. The male dancer is certainly an athlete and a good way for the uninitiated viewer to take a first look at ballet is by enjoying the *danseur* as an athlete. In the matter of stamina, physical energy and muscular control a male dancer is as powerful and far more rigorously-trained than most of the athletes we may see in the Olympics or in a hard-fought football game.

The dancer's secret on stage is that effort, strain and even strength have to be concealed in the cause of an artistic impression. But anyone who has watched dancers in class, or seen a male dancer in the wings of a theatre after a particularly exhausting solo or *pas de deux*, will be aware that the physical demands made upon him are prodigious. (Some indication of just how taxing is the dancer's work can even be judged on stage, when a rain of sweat can be seen spraying out from a dancer as he pirouettes.) A simple comparative test of physical endurance between a dancer and an athlete is found in the role of male dancer as partner. In many ballets he is required to carry the ballerina high above his head, sometimes in a one-arm lift, with all the appearance of nonchalance. It is difficult perhaps for the audience to understand that he is lifting a woman who may weigh anything up to 110 or 120 pounds.

The demands upon the dancer's body and the athlete's are exactly the same, in that both require muscles to be trained and exceptional skill to be used in the acquisition of strength, stamina and speed. The difference comes in the visual expression of these qualities, for the dancer's body has in the main always to appear aesthetically pleasing. Ballet is an art, and certain rules about proportion and line must apply. Before he becomes a dancer a young man has to conform to certain laws pertaining to his appearance. The head must be well placed on a reasonably long neck; the trunk must be well shaped, the legs must provide a proper length to sustain an essential harmony of form, and the muscles must in their training avoid any appearance of overdevelopment: no male dancer could seem so indulgently bulging as a weight-lifter or body builder.

The boy who wants to become a dancer will never be accepted into a major ballet school if he is ill-proportioned, if his legs are too short, his head too large or his back too long. More important, he will be given a rigorous medical examination to see that there is no inherent weakness (or even possibility of weakness) in his physical frame. Some schools have to reject otherwise-promising applicants who want to become ballet dancers because doctors and physiotherapists have detected indications that strain or injury would result from ballet training because of some seemingly minor weakness in a knee or a joint. Athletes train very hard, and over the past few decades much more emphasis has been put on a systematic and scientific study of their skills. One of the reasons for the success of Soviet athletes is that they are so seriously and carefully prepared for competitions. The dancer's training is the result of 300 years of practical study and development, during which the language of the classic academic dance, the *danse d'école*, has emerged, been codified and refined.

The dancers' daily class is a ritual which has to be undertaken every morning of their professional lives. Its purpose, as the youngest student in the first class in a ballet school realises, is to tune the body, and throughout the professional career the same routine of bends and stretches, of warming muscles and ligaments, must be undergone. It is a careful process, it is a slow process. And it is a process which has grown up over the centuries. It combines scientific principles and the wisdom of those centuries. It has been said that if a dancer does not take class for one day he will know it; class missed for two days means that his colleagues will notice; class missed for three days and the public will notice, and the dancer cannot dance. This daily tuning of the body, this quest for a state of physical wellbeing and preparedness, is very hard for the general public to understand. But it is only the preparation for the more important work that fills the rest of the day for a professional dancer. It prepares the dancer for rehearsal, and there will be a further 'warm up' class immediately before the performance begins. (One of the greatest risks any dancer can take is to go on stage with the body 'cold'.)

Young boys in the ballet school in Kazakhstan. These are fourth-year pupils in one of the many ballet schools which now exist in each of the republics of the Soviet Union.

The delicate balance implicit between the dancer as a technical athlete and as artist is something which concerns many male dancers. The distinguished Icelandic dancer Helgi Tomasson, a star of the New York City Ballet, has observed that 'technique should only be a means to achieve something else; it is the instrument, not the end. I don't want the audience to come to the theatre and say, "He doesn't jump as high as someone else", or "He turns more than someone else". That kind of audience makes it harder for the male dancer to be accepted for what he really is. He is not a kind of athlete but a special kind of artist.'

Yet athleticism is vital to the work of the dancer, and the exhilaration of physical prowess – huge jumps, a multitude of turns – is what the public immediately applauds and what the dancer is called upon to display. Helgi Tomasson makes a valid point about the desire of commentators, eager to introduce a larger public to ballet, to stress that male dancing is a form of athletics. Speaking in *Dance Perspectives* No. 40 he has said, 'I think the Americans have been perhaps saying too much about a dancer being like an athlete. Yes, it does take a tremendous amount of physical work, but ballet is an art.

Dancer as athlete: Denys Ganio in the boxing solo made by Roland Petit for this leading dancer of the Ballet National de Marseille.

We should try to have it accepted on those terms. I think people know enough about the activity side of it now. So let's start thinking about what it is as an art. Audiences . . . watch a fine male dancer showing the purity and simplicity of classical dancing, and they act as if they wanted him to do something else, something spectacular, to show that he is good. Do they want him to go out there with a bat? We should push to be accepted for what we are as artists.'

But it is inevitable that the artistry which, as Helgi Tomasson indicates, is of prime concern for the male dancer, must be sustained by physical excellence. A dancer as artist is the prisoner of his body if he cannot make it do his bidding. His daily concern in class is with the ultra-refined athleticism of the classic ballet. Some dancers are prepared to go to gymnastic training to extend their strength for certain arduous ballets in which there may be a great deal of difficult lifting and partnering of the ballerina – a training which can be dangerous if muscles become overdeveloped. In ballet, the ideal is for a long and harmoniously-developed musculature; bulging, bunchy muscles are not pleasing to see in the theatre.

The athlete as dancer. The Pilobolus Dance Theatre began when a group of American college students decided to bring their physical skills into dance. Its movement style provides a combination of gymnastics and modern dance and the result is a performance manner which is acrobatic and marked by extreme muscular control.

Similarly, dancers are able to offer their balletic skill as a help to athletes, and athletes can always benefit from ballet training. The academic dance has always sought muscular efficiency, and athletes can increase their performance potential when shown by a ballet teacher how effort may be set to maximum effect and energy conserved for moments of maximum expenditure. Skaters, skiers, gymnasts, sometimes even football players, have learned that ballet training will, in the first instance, help them to analyse their actions and develop great technical finesse in their sport. The dance teacher Andrew Hardie devised a handbook, *Ballet Exercises for Athletes*, which was produced for the Amateur Athletics Association in collaboration with the Royal Academy of Dancing, and in 1956 there began an experiment in adapting ballet exercises for athletes which highlighted the possibilities for helpful collaboration. The unprecedented success of John Curry as a skater, winner of Olympic gold medals and the World Skating Championship in 1976, owed something to his love and understanding of ballet and his appreciation of dance training. He took skating away from the ice rink and into the world of dance. Watching Curry – and certain great Soviet skaters – we see how like dancing skating has become; it is truly now to be called ice dancing.

Perhaps no more pertinent comment about the physical demands of dancing and the concomitant alertness of the dancer can be found than the observation made by Hugh McIlvanney in *The Observer*, 28 November 1976, reviewing the book *Michener on Sport*: 'Dr James Nicholas, orthopaedic specialist to the New York Jets football team identified twenty-one components of an athletic act, grouping them into three categories: neuro-muscular-physical (endurance, reaction time); mental-psychometric (intelligence, alertness); environmental (playing conditions, equipment). He then applied those criteria to sixty-one different sports and made ratings of their demands. Dr Nicholas did not examine *Tour de France* cycling, but he placed prize-fighting, basketball, American football and ice hockey particularly high. One of the more interesting conclusions was to put ballet right up there with those punishing games, appreciably ahead of soccer and fencing.'

Left: The skater as dancer. It was John Curry who revealed the virtuoso skater as artist. For many years ice skating had flirted with various ideas of 'art' and entertainment, from the days of Sonja Henie, the Norwegian star who charmed a new public in films in the 1940s. Curry, both World and Olympic champion, has alone been able to show that ice dancing is a credible art form, not least by his decision to use the finest music and to enlist the help of such choreographers as Twyla Tharp, Kenneth MacMillan, Peter Darrell and John Butler.

Right: A footballer jumps with maximum evidence of energy. Diego Maradoña, the Argentinian star.

One of the first hurdles that a male dancer has to overcome, however, is the fact of *being* a male dancer, of persuading friends and family that the career is not as dire as traditional prejudice would make it seem, and that neither his masculinity nor his athletic ability is in question. In *Dance Perspectives* No. 1, Lincoln Kirstein, chief architect of the School of American Ballet and of the New York City Ballet, wrote of this problem as it existed twenty-five years ago. 'In America, where skills at speculative ball-games are fixed at a premium past any other human capacity, dancing to good music on stage has an effete smell. A talented youth, unless he comes from a theatrical or musical family, or one so low in the social structure that even dancing is some sort of advancement, must kill his parents, symbolically at least, if he is finally to achieve his heart's desire. It would be better for most artists, except novelists, to be orphans. For the Dance there is the crucial moment in the ritual encounter: "Son, if you persist in this folly you will Kill Your Mother." Mother rarely allows the same for Dad, but it would be more honest if she did. The worst of it is that by the time Son has had the sense to blast this blackmail, the guts to leave home and get a job operating an elevator to pay for his lessons, he will be too old to profit by them. The very few brilliant (i.e. well-trained) male dancers bred in the West have all had, by some fluke or another, ten or more years of hard training before they were twenty . . . The prejudice against male dancing (which never extends to high-paid performers in variety, TV, Films or Broadway, or to visiting British or Russians) has its roots in the position of the Ballerina in the last century.'

Kirstein's point is underlined by the comment of the American dancer Ted Kivitt which appeared in *Dancers on Dancing* by Cynthia Lyle (Drake Publishers Inc., New York 1977), 'My mother took me to my first dance lessons when I was seven years old – tap dancing and acrobatics . . . At age ten I started taking ballet lessons, but only with the understanding that I would take private lessons and that none of my friends would find out. So my mother found a teacher and arranged it so that only three people were allowed in the studio with me: the teacher, the pianist and my mother . . . The first thing I ever did on stage was *Le Spectre de la Rose*. I was about twelve or thirteen. That was another traumatic experience, because the moment I stepped out the kids started whistling and calling me names . . . These were smart-assed kids who though I was a fairy and did not know what was going on. I started to come down with asthma again. Kids at my elementary school called me a sissy and a fairy, and my best friend turned against me.'

Ted Kivitt wrote about the climate of feeling in the mid-1950s. It is highly significant that in the thirty years since then a very considerable revolution in public attitudes towards dancing, and especially male dancing, has taken place. In that time the dance audience has massively increased – in the United States of America it is estimated as exceeding twelve million – and the efforts of companies to present educational programmes, and the influence of television, have wiped away a lot of prejudice and suggested to the young generations that dancing has much to offer as a career.

Since Kirstein wrote his *Dance Perspectives* article from which we have quoted, the situation in America has massively changed. His own School of American Ballet recruits young boys by means of scholarships from all around the United States and now has a larger intake of boys and young men than ever before in its fifty-year history. The same is true of Britain. The chief ballet school in the country is the Royal Ballet School. Its junior school, at White Lodge in Richmond Park, is, with the Menuhin Music School, one of the only two 'prestige' schools in the country recognised by the Department of Education, which automatically gives a direct grant to any child accepted on audition. This has meant that boys no longer have to justify the necessity of grant aid from a local authority in order to learn to dance. The increase in the number of boys attending White Lodge has been remarkable. The annual Royal Ballet School matinee at the Royal Opera House, Covent Garden, always includes items danced by the young boys at the Lower School. Their energy and alertness and their evident joy in what they are dancing, as well as their physical prowess, should make any parent proud.

Lincoln Kirstein's observation that some boys may come too late to ballet raises several very interesting points. In classical ballet, as distinct from contemporary dance and other forms of theatre or social dance, it is usual for a boy to start training at about the age of eleven. An earlier beginning is possible but not always advisable: younger boys, often slower physical developers than girls, do not always have joints and bones strong enough to sustain the rigorous discipline and the physical stresses that must inevitably come with proper training. Recruitment for the great ballet schools (the Royal Ballet School, the schools attached to the Kirov, the Bolshoi, the Paris Opéra, the Royal Danish Ballet School and the School of American Ballet) requires both boys and girls to be ten or eleven years old at their first audition. Auditioning is a very thorough process, not only in matters of physique but also in its concern with natural aptitude and intelligence. This rigorous selection also examines family characteristics in judging and predicting the child's physical development: whether, for instance he will grow to a suitable height. This is the first of the continuing series of assessments that mark the young student's progress through the whole of his balletic training, since this weeding out process is ultimately an act of kindness. Arnold Haskell, when Director of the Royal Ballet School, once observed that it was better to face a few tears at the age of twelve than heartbreak at eighteen.

No matter what national differences there exist between the various schools in London, Paris, New York, Russia or Copenhagen, the ultimate aim and the ultimate process is the same. The universality of ballet as a theatrical language means that if a television camera goes into any of these great schools the picture of students in class will be recognisably similar throughout the world. The Royal Ballet School provides an immediate example of the system. It is divided into an Upper and Lower School. The Lower School at White Lodge – a former Royal residence in Richmond Park, Surrey – deals with students between the ages of eleven and sixteen. Its concern is both with balletic training and with the necessary academic education of the young up to GCE O Level. Pupils are accepted for an initial trial period of a year, and those who are obliged through some physical weakness to leave can easily be transferred into the ordinary secondary educational system.

Boy students at the School of American Ballet in New York. Above: advanced students are working at the barre in the special men's class. Right: younger boys are making their first jumps: already the rules of beautiful positioning of the body in the air are being recognised.

Two more views of the students at work in The School of American Ballet. Above: Peter Boal, a recent graduate into New York City Ballet, is seen in the boys' class in *attitude*. Right: The young boy students are learning the essential art of partnering.

At White Lodge the academic education is rounded, but the overriding concern is the training of the pupil in the disciplines of the classic academic dance. This is done through carefully regulated daily class and through such associated concerns as folk dancing, music – so vital to the later career – and a certain amount of weight training as a preparation for the eventual demands of partnering.

At the end of their five years at White Lodge those who have completed their course and are thought suitable for further training make the transition to the Upper School. Their physical and technical progress as dancers is by this time considerable, thanks to the fact of working in an environment where male dancing is not something 'special' but a commonplace fact of life. A boy's progress under these circumstances is much faster and more secure than that of a boy who has been forced to work in a school where he may be the sole boy among a bevy of girls. Helgi Tomasson, describing his own schooldays in Iceland, noted: 'When I started to dance I was ten and I was the only boy

In the School of the Moscow Boshoi Ballet, Mikhail Gabovich is seen in the late 1950s taking a men's class. Among his pupils, far right, is Vladimir Vasiliev.

in our national theatre school, though there were 250 girls. I enjoyed the music and I enjoyed the movement, but I was not really serious about becoming a dancer until after I had spent a summer at the ballet school in Copenhagen when I was sixteen. There, for the first time, I was in competition. I had never seen boys of my age dancing before. That summer I decided I wanted to become a dancer. In Copenhagen I was not teased about dancing the way I had been in Reykjavik. It got around my school at home that I was the only boy in the ballet class at the theatre, so I was teased by the other boys and also by the girls.' (*Dance Perspectives* No. 40.)

Once into the Upper School, the demands of professionalism and the nearness of possible graduation into the company (not all the boys get into the Royal Ballet; many find a career in other troupes or in other forms of theatre) is an added stimulus to endeavour. And once into the company, the real rigours of dancing as a career begin to be felt.

Right: Vladimir Vasiliev in his solo from the *Don Quixote* pas de deux. Vasiliev's dancing is celebrated for its bravura and its academic rectitude. His dancing thrills the public by his power to consume space, and also by the generosity of his temperament.

Above: Demonstration is one of the secrets of fine teaching. Here Voinov is shown with a boys' class at the Kirov demonstrating a *plié* in fifth position.

In the field of contemporary dance the rules and precedence are different. Early training is not a prerequisite, though an athletic and supple body is an immediate advantage. Such important performers as Paul Taylor or Robert Cohan came late to the actualities of contemporary training, Taylor having been a college athlete and Cohan having returned from military service with the US Army before attending class at the Martha Graham School. We must note, though, that late beginners were more an historical fact of modern dance than a present tradition. It is one of the most fascinating aspects of the work of contemporary dance companies and the support that has been given to contemporary dance in the educational system in the United States and in Britain that nowadays many more young men become aware early of the artistic and physical fulfilment to be found in dancing. The increased popularity of dancing in all its forms has

Robert Cohan giving class to members of the London Contemporary Dance Theatre.

also meant that the old prejudices against dance (prejudices, though, which still attach to the word 'ballet') are fading fast and young men see nothing peculiar in the idea of dance as a career. Of particular significance is the success initiated by Robert Cohan in London in 1967 when he was invited to found a school and a company to bring Graham technique to Britain. The result of the subsequent tours by the London Contemporary Dance Company, and Cohan's insistence on taking dance into colleges and schools for educational purposes, and the strength of the image of the male dancer presented by the company, was to show to many young men the wonderful possibilities of dancing as a physically creative career. A work such as Cohan's *Class*, with its stunning physical virtuosity and the power and the virility of the male dancing superbly displayed, must excite much admiration and a desire to emulate these feats.

Patrick Harding-Irmer of London Contemporary Dance Theatre in Robert Cohan's *Class*.

Paul Taylor began dancing late. While studying art at university, and enjoying an athletic career, he made first contact with dance and received scholarships to the Juilliard School in New York and the Graham School, and also the ballet school of the Metropolitan Opera House. In 1953 at the age of twenty-three he made his first appearances with the companies of Pearl Lang and Merce Cunningham, and soon started creating his own dances. His powerful physique was allied to a remarkable lightness and ease of movement, and these qualities were uniquely effective in the dance pieces which he made during the 1950s and 1960s. He danced in the 1950s with Martha Graham and is seen above with Helen McGehee in Graham's *Acrobats of God*; he formed his own permanent ensemble in 1961 and is seen top right with his company in *Orbs*, a masterpiece of modern dance.

Right: This action shot by Anthony Crickmay conveys the energy and the technical brilliance of the men in the Martha Graham company which Graham herself used in her *Secular Games* of 1962. Taken from the wings, this picture shows Robert Powell (right) roaring on to the stage. Powell was a dancer of exceptionally feline grace and power.

JACK MITCH

A great dancer of an earlier generation, Igor Youskevitch – whose beautiful classic dancing was essentially aristocratic – came to ballet by way of sports training. He speaks with particular sympathy about the problems of a young man wanting to take up dancing: 'I am always tempted to give moral support to those young men who would like to dance because there are still some who question the compatibility of this desire with masculinity. The answer, to the best of my knowledge, is that a masculine wish to dance connotes a desire to move in order to express and create as opposed to the female's propensity for losing herself in music and rhythm for the joy of physical revelation . . . For a man the technical or athletic side of dance is a rational challenge. Once mastered, it provides him with an opportunity to display strength, skill and endurance, as well as with the vocabulary and means to achieve creativity. Those who hesitate to enter the profession, fearing it is not manly, should ask themselves: Is it acceptable for a man to sing or paint or write poetry? If it is, then what could be a greater challenge for him than to combine all of these arts in himself; in his body and through his movements to create them all?' (*Dance Perspectives* No. 40.)

Twyla Tharp's *Brahms' Paganini* is a virtuoso work which begins with a very demanding solo for a male dancer. It was superbly created by William Whitener, who is seen here.

John Carrafa, Raymond Kurshals and Tom Rawe in Twyla Tharp's *The Fugue*. *The Fugue* is danced without music; it is a highly organised and very complicated exercise in stamped rhythm which requires the most intense rapport between the members of its cast. It was originally danced by three women, but these three men gave extraordinarily vivid and exciting performances.

Previous page: Patrick Dupond in a characteristic soaring jump in rehearsal at the Paris Opéra. This ornate setting epitomises the grandeur and spaciousness of the palace designed by Charles Garnier, which opened in 1875.

Below: Robert Kovich and Chris Komar of the Merce Cunningham Dance Company in *Fractions*. The clarity of the dance image of those two fine artists is typical of the austere beauty of Cunningham's work at its best.

Right: *The Sunday Times* of 17 July 1983 carried this picture of Darshan Bhuller of the London Contemporary Dance Theatre, noting that he had just received an Arts Council bursary to return to his old school in Leeds to choreograph a dance work for the students. Harehills Middle School in Leeds has had the imagination to provide compulsory dance lessons for every boy and girl in the school. In this school's policy we see an important recognition by an educational authority of the potential of dance to help educate and extend the awareness of the young. Other schools – though still too few – have in recent years become aware of the value of dance in the curriculum. Darshan Bhuller's teacher, Nadine Senior, made a most illuminating comment to *The Sunday Times*: 'He was good enough to be a professional footballer, so when he became a dancer that made it OK for the other lads. He always comes back to teach when he is performing in Leeds and all the kids idolise him.'

A different strand of dancing for boys is no less apparent in what are known as vocational schools – those schools which prepare dancers for careers in the theatre and which offer all-round training in the performing arts. (Perhaps the best known today is the School of Performing Arts in New York, whose students were the model for the enormously successful television programme *Fame*.) Twenty years ago these schools were predominantly concerned with young girls aspiring to careers in the theatre. Today these vocational schools have separate boys' departments which cater for the vastly increased intake of young men eager to try their luck in the theatre.

An important contributory fact seems the remarkable expansion of Disco dancing. Anyone watching Disco dancing must be aware that it makes very considerable physical demands upon the dancer, and the virtuosity – and it is virtuosity – which can be seen in Discos inevitably reflects the young generation's increased awareness about many forms of theatrical dancing. We can see young men and women spinning in multiple pirouettes and vying with each other in bravura effects. Many of these brilliant steps have come from observation of theatrical dance, and the Disco dancers are often aware that their performances could be further improved by some form of professional training. There results from this a first introduction to the disciplines of a dance school, and in some cases this leads to a decision to make a career of what had been a hobby and a pastime. It is an interesting sidelight upon the conditions for the young in society today, where so tragically many are victims of unemployment and lack of job opportunities, that dancing has become both a refuge and a release. In vocational schools, or even in part-time instruction in community centres, the young find a framework and a discipline which they can comprehend and which seems to offer some hope for the future.

An additional attraction for young men who decide to take up dancing as a career is the increased job opportunities for male dancers. There has traditionally always been a huge surplus of girl dancers chasing too few jobs – it is not unusual for 300 girls to attend an audition for a handful of vacancies in a ballet company or a musical show – but there are few problems in finding work for a well trained and willing young male dancer.

The directors of many vocational schools have told us that the pressures upon their students are so considerable, and the training so broad in its range, that anything less than full attention and total effort is unacceptable. In the matter of boys, the rule seems to be that laziness or indifference can only lead to dismissal, but the boy who works hard and responds to training can still be assured of work on leaving school: the demand for male dancers throughout the world still outruns the supply. (We have phone calls from ballet companies in Europe asking us if we know of 'any good young male soloists' – to which the answer is inevitably 'yes, but they are all contracted to major companies'.)

A dancer's initial training can vary from the seven years spent in the ballet school of a major company to the intensive three or four years required in the contemporary dance idiom. Thereafter come the years of daily practice which are the absolute basic requirement for a career in the theatre; the hard work that is going to make a student a better dancer and bring technical improvement is an additional task. It is perhaps worth reiterating that the dancer is the only adult who subjects himself daily to classroom disciplines, and who understands that his commercial and technical existence require him to submit himself to the beady eye and constant correction of a teacher throughout his professional performing career.

Although certain other executant performers – pianists, violinists, even singers – need to practise and study throughout their careers, and although athletes must always maintain a rigorous training schedule, dancers alone can never relax and escape the watchful gaze of a teacher who corrects the greatest performers as strictly as the newest apprentice. Humility in face of the physical aspects of the art is an essential of a dancer's career.

Once that career is over and a dancer has to accept the decline of his physical powers – by the time he is forty, when muscles lose their resilience and the body itself rejects the punishing work it has undergone for over twenty years in the theatre – the male dancer (like the female dancer) is faced with a mid-life crisis of having to decide upon a new channel for his energies and a new source of income. For men especially there often comes a moment in their twenties when, entirely realistically, they can see that a dancing career will never bring either the financial rewards or the artistic satisfaction they had hoped for. Rather than opt for years of work in a *corps de ballet* they bravely decide to make a new beginning while youth is on their side, rechannelling themselves into anything from insurance to television directing. For those who decide to retain their links with dancing there comes the question of teaching dance. Some dancers open schools of their own or join the teaching faculty of their parent company. In Britain, the Royal Academy of Dancing has for a decade run a unique one-year Professional Dancer's Training Course, which is available only to dancers who have given up a professional stage career and need to acquire the skills necessary for teaching students of all ages and all levels of ability. In the still-expanding world of dance teaching, where of the many thousands of children who attend a ballet class only a few may go on to a professional dancing career, it is yet very important that the young are brought in contact with the essentially theatrical nature of the art they are learning – under a professional dancer they must inevitably become aware of their basic *pliés* and *tendus* are part of the great vocabulary of theatre dance, and that as they perform them they share the same muscular experience as Baryshnikov or Makarova.

Right: Hans Beck and Adeline Genée in the pas de deux from Bournonville's *Flower Festival in Genzano*. This turn-of-the-century photograph offers indication of that parity between artists, and that courteous companionship, which is so essentially a part of the relationship between men and women in Bournonville's ballets. Adeline Genée, Danish born and trained, had her greatest triumphs in London and America but returned to Copenhagen from time to time to dance with Hans Beck.

Courteous Companionship: the Dancer as Partner

A man dancing will have to go far beyond entertainment. A man dancing will somehow have to stand for what a man can become. He will really have to be a hero, in his body, his mind, his spirit. . . . The man dancing in the theatre is the image of man as he performs the rite of being a man for all men in the audience.

Erick Hawkins, 'Why does a man dance?' *The Dance Experience* (Universe Books, New York)

The traditional view of the male partner is of the man as a princely, noble cavalier, supporting the ballerina but keeping somewhat in the background. This is a portrait of the man as we see him in the nineteenth century ballets and it came about through the emergence of the ballerina as the dominant figure in Romantic ballet. The male dancer was seen as her lover and admirer, or her victim, but his more practical function was to provide an extension for her technical skills. Supported by the man the ballerina could balance for a greater length of time, could spin in supported turns, could be held hovering gently over the earth so as to seem weightless, and could be effortlessly lifted so that she might become increasingly a creature of the air. Her *pointe* shoes were an implicit comment upon her minimal contact with the earth; through her partner's ministrations she appeared even more a denizen of the air and ultimately even more unreal as a woman.

The partnership between these artists was not that of equals. At a time when women in society had little or no separate legal identity, the stage image offered a related view of women, but with one great contrast – a disproportionate concentration on the ballerina at the expense of her partner. The ballets themselves were spectacles designed for a male audience, and the woman on display was shown as either a fantasy figure or an ornament.

The difference in today's partnerships is immense, since the entire sexual orientation of ballet has changed. Of course, in current presentations of the nineteenth-century repertory we still see the old attitudes underlying the relationship between the hero and the heroine in the *pas de deux*. In *Swan Lake*, *The Sleeping Beauty* or *Giselle*, no matter what additional opportunities the production may offer the male dancer, the ballerina is still the dominant figure and must be respected as such. It is the function of the man today, as when the ballets were created, to present the ballerina to the greatest advantage – to be both lover and pillar of strength. Certain celebrated partnerships were initially created in these ballets, and we have but to think of one of the great dance partnerships of this century, that of Alicia Markova and Anton Dolin, to understand the extraordinary emotional and physical rapport which is necessary even in the old ballets. Dolin's art as a partner lay in the generosity and elegance with which he showed off his ballerina. Utterly secure in the mechanics of double work, he contrived to suggest a complete absorption in what his partner was doing and an absolute sympathy with her feelings. With the crystalline, floating Markova he gave the impression that he was not so much lifting her into the air as preventing her from flying away, and with many other ballerinas his range of artistry earned him a reputation as a prince among partners.

Right: Alicia Markova and Anton Dolin in *Princess Aurora* – American Ballet Theatre's staging of the last act of *The Sleeping Beauty* – in the early 1940s. The nobility with which Dolin is presenting Markova is reflected not only in his obvious pride in his ballerina but also in her serene confidence in his presence. This was an ideal classical partnership.

Below: Giselle's death, with the illustrious Alicia Markova partnered by Erik Bruhn. In the spring of 1955, Markova, one of the greatest Giselles of this century, had returned to American Ballet Theatre at the old Metropolitan Opera House, New York, and was scheduled to dance with Igor Youskevitch. An extra matinée was put into the season to allow more people to see Markova, and characteristically she chose to dance with the young Erik Bruhn who had never appeared as Albrecht before. There resulted an incandescent performance, and our action photograph by Fred Fehl captures an essential fact of memorable interpretations such as this – the mysterious rapport which exists between artists. This spiritual communion is as essential to great partnerships as the physical understanding. (Fred Fehl, the Vienna-born American photographer, habitually photographed ballet from the prompt box of the old Metropolitan Opera House in New York – hence the unusual camera angle.)

Rare indeed have been partnerships as theatrically convincing or as lasting – they danced together for thirty years – as that of Markova and Dolin. The physical sympathy between two dancers, the sense in which they become entirely aware of each other's reactions, the way in which each seems a theatrical extension of the other, can only result from long periods of study, great thought and an acute sense of the theatrical image which they must present together. Today's ballet companies rarely afford the opportunities or the time necessary to develop such collaborative art. Previous generations were able to admire the long-standing and potent theatrical companionship of Alexandra Danilova and Frederic Franklin, or of Alicia Alonso and Igor Youskevitch. For nearly twenty years Margot Fonteyn worked with Robert Helpmann, but in today's ballet there are few partnerships which have endured so long, and imprinted themselves thereby upon the public consciousness: the four most convincing in recent years have been those of the Stuttgart stars Marcia Haydée and Richard Cragun; the celebrated Bolshoi couple Ekaterina Maximova and Vladimir Vasiliev; the Royal Ballet's Antoinette Sibley and Anthony Dowell; and New York City Ballet's Peter Martins and Suzanne Farrell.

Above: Vladimir Vasiliev is seen with his wife Ekaterina Maximova in the pas de deux from the second act of *Giselle*.

Right: Alexandra Danilova and Frederic Franklin in Balanchine's *Danses Concertantes* as staged for the Ballet Russe de Monte Carlo in designs by Eugene Berman. In modern and classic roles this great partnership led the Ballet Russe de Monte Carlo and won converts to ballet on tours of the United States during the 1940s and 1950s.

Jerome Robbins's *Afternoon of a Faun* is a brilliant reworking of the Nijinsky *L'Après-midi d'un faune*, using the Debussy music but transferring the action to a New York ballet studio, and providing entirely new choreography. The faun is now a young dance student; Nijinsky's nymphs have become a single girl ballet student. Their meeting is shown as if reflected in the mirror that lines a dance studio wall. Sibley and Dowell, stars of the Royal Ballet and ideally matched in temperament and schooling, brought their own magic to a ballet which was originally created for the New York City Ballet Company.

A partnership requires the most intense sympathy between the ballerina and the male dancer if it is to work properly, a sympathy that is emotional as well as physical, and may often spring from a shared experience in training and schooling as dancers. Sometimes two dancers will find that they are happily partners because of a similarity of physique or of dance style. In Nicholas Dromgoole's *Sibley and Dowell* (Collins; London; 1976) the two dancers discussed their work and in talking about partnership Anthony Dowell observed that their common success was more a matter of sympathy, having the same feelings, of understanding each other. 'The physical side is important, we have to match each other, in height and proportion and learn to move in sympathy with each other, but there has to be a mental and an emotional sympathy as well. When we share so much of our professional lives we are really sharing our hopes, our successes, our miseries and depressions. . . . Having danced so much together, . . . we have built up a terrific emotional relationship which works so well on stage, the shock of not having it would be very hard, and dancing is hard enough anyway.'

Sibley and Dowell, products of the Royal Ballet School, and Maximova and Vasiliev of the Bolshoi's School, typify partnerships which start with the initial bond of a shared education. Sometimes, though, there is an implicit contrast between partners, with differences of age or of schooling, that yet strikes the theatrical spark. This is what happened with Margot Fonteyn when, at the age of forty-one, she found a new partner in the twenty-two-year-old defector from the Kirov Ballet, Rudolf Nureyev. Their backgrounds were very dissimilar but their combined temperaments on stage – Fonteyn's reserved and musical manner and her dramatic sensitivity; Nureyev's physical fire and his no less fiery temperament – resulted in an emotional and physical magic which was vastly to the public taste and became headline news.

The most potent image of this stage relationship was created by Frederick Ashton, who cast the two stars as the doomed lovers of *Marguerite and Armand*, and displayed Fonteyn's maturity illuminated by the blaze of Nureyev's youthful ardour. In certain cases a partnership can be nurtured and shaped by a choreographer, and this was the case in Stuttgart, where John Cranko was able to unite the artistry of his ballerina Marcia Haydée with that of his young American *premier danseur*, Richard Cragun. In ballets as diverse as *The Taming of the Shrew*, which was created for them, and *Romeo and Juliet*, there emerged a collaborative and intensely 'aware' relationship which strengthened with the years. Truly these two artists could seem to dance as one, and in minor works the very fact of their partnership seemed to enhance entirely ordinary choreography.

Yet, though a choreographer as perceptive as Cranko could see how two artists might form a partnership, there is no rule which can turn two dancers into a team. There is a secret chemistry which has to work on an emotional level as well as a sense in which the two bodies respond one to the other in dance. Nadia Nerina has noted that she found an immediate physical sympathy with Alexis Rassine because of their muscular similarity, and commenting on their partnership Rassine noted: 'We danced together instinctively; we were alike in physique and we had an instant muscular rapport which meant we worked without problems.'

There is, too, a physical chemistry which must be the result of ceaseless work to make partnering seem effortless, spontaneous and convincing. Bad partnering can destroy a ballerina's performance; good partnering can sometimes raise an indifferent *danseuse* to heights she would not otherwise reach. Thus fine partners are treasured by ballerinas, and certain distinguished *danseurs* have gained reputations, over and above their individual artistry, as exceptional partners no matter with whom they are dancing. Like Anton Dolin, Desmond Kelly and Donald MacLeary of the Royal Ballet and Ivan Nagy, lately with American Ballet Theatre, have earned the respect and affection of every ballerina whom they have partnered because of the sense of security they give in double work, and because of their dignity and distinction as artists. On stage as in society there is a quality of good manners that is expected of the male dancer, which in the theatre has been defined by Lincoln Kirstein as a kind of 'superhuman courtesy'.

Above: Margot Fonteyn and Rudolf Nureyev in *Marguerite and Armand*. Ashton's ballet of 1963 encapsulated the partnership of these two stars.
Right: Fonteyn and Nureyev in the Kingdom of Shades scene from Petipa's *La Bayadère* as staged by the Royal Ballet.

Above: Desmond Kelly and Deanne Bergsma in the Royal Ballet's production of Glen Tetley's *Field Figures*. The acrobatic nature of such modern partnering is exemplified in this picture.

Right: Natalia Makarova and Ivan Nagy of American Ballet Theatre in Fokine's *The Firebird*. The partnership here is one of captor and captive, as the Tsarevitch Ivan attempts to prevent the magic bird from flying away, and Fokine achieved great dramatic power from this conflict between the ballerina and her danseur in this extended duet.

Far right: Natalia Makarova and Anthony Dowell in the second act of *Giselle* with the Royal Ballet in 1980. The ballerina's total confidence in the arms of her partner, and a common sympathy for the drama, allow the dancers to recapture an essential image of Romanticism: the ghost of Giselle here seems as impalpable as night mist.

There are two qualities which mark a great partnership. The first is the complex matter of physical accord, in which the two bodies may seem to 'think' as one; the second is the no less important matter of creating an emotional and dramatic ambiance in which the two bodies seem to 'feel' as one. This is as difficult as the creation of any physical rapport, and it presupposes that the two artists will find each other mutually inspiring and will be able to relive the traditional love scenes or dramatic moments of the old ballets with renewed enthusiasm at every moment. In some well-known partnerships this magic never failed: in *Giselle*, for example, Markova and Dolin were as totally persuasive in the joy and pathos of the first act as in the moonlit mystery of the second. Certain other artists today seek to find a fresh image for each performance, and we recall with gratitude the variously different but always compelling performances of *Swan Lake* or *Giselle* which we have seen from Natalia Makarova and Anthony Dowell. There is an element of risk-taking in partnerships in which, however well the two dancers may know each other, they must be prepared to accept that one or other may go off into what may seem flights of fantasy. Of course the steps are a bedrock of unchanging exactness, but nevertheless an artist responds as a human being to emotional impulses, and in performances by Lynn Seymour and Christopher Gable we have seen how they appeared swept along as MacMillan's Romeo and Juliet on a gust of youthful passion which seemed to catch them both with complete spontaneity.

The dramatic demands of a *pas de deux* are varied, and there is no better example of the range possible than the series of duets with which the Archduke Rudolf in Kenneth MacMillan's *Mayerling* confronts each of the women in his life. In the first act of the ballet we see the celebrations of Rudolf's wedding with Princess Stephanie of Belgium, at a ball in the Royal Palace of the Hofburg. Rudolf is not enamoured of his bride; we see him reunited during the ball with the Countess Larisch, who has been his mistress and who is both an evil genius to him and also the only woman to understand him. The role was admirably created by Merle Park and in this first duet with Rudolf (David Wall) we sense both her continuing passion for him and his mixture of reliance and rejection. In a subsequent scene Rudolf makes for his mother's apartments. The Empress Elisabeth, a role created by Georgina Parkinson, is entirely unable to cope with her son's desire for affection and sympathy, and she frigidly rejects his every appeal – MacMillan shows these by Rudolf seeking to lay his head on his mother's lap, and then trying to entwine himself round her – and the duet offers images which invert all the usual attitudes of a *pas de deux*, since here the woman is reluctant even to be touched by the man, an unrequited affection rather than requited love its theme.

The first act ends with the wedding night encounter of Rudolf and his innocent young bride. Here all the passion and despair that Rudolf has pent up pours out in a brutal assault upon a young woman – Rudolf, having been victim of Larisch and his mother, now makes Stephanie his victim in turn. He first terrifies her with a skull and a pistol, omens of his fascination with death, and he then physically terrorises her. The choreography becomes hectic and almost hysterical, reflecting Stephanie's horrified appeals to him for compassion, and the acrobatic nature of the dance shows the young

In Kenneth MacMillan's *Mayerling*, the key to the character of the Archduke Rudolf lies in his relationship with a variety of women, which inspires a sequence of very revealing pas de deux. Here David Wall is seen in the role of the Archduke with Merle Park as his mistress, the Countess Larisch . . .

. . . and here (left to right) with Georgina Parkinson as his mother, the Empress Elisabeth ; with Laura Connor as his mistress, Mitzi Caspar, in a tavern ; with Wendy Ellis as his new bride, Stephanie, on their wedding night, when he terrifies her with a pistol and a skull ; with Lynn Seymour as Maria Vetsera.

princess (an outstanding portrait by Wendy Ellis) flinging herself at Rudolf and being caught and thrown as if at the mercy of some terrifying storm. MacMillan's choreography has a penetrating power to suggest the furthest reaches of human frailty and human desire, in images that seem explicit but are in fact highly poetic symbols of psychic attitudes. Just as in the rape scene in *The Invitation* of two decades previously he shows the motivation and deepest feelings of his characters through his extension of the classical academic technique. Duets like these demand physical daring from both dancers, and an emotional daring which will allow them to give themselves to the choreography while also remaining entirely in control of its effects.

In the second act of *Mayerling*, seven years after his marriage, we see Rudolf enjoying himself in a low tavern with one of his mistresses, Mitzi Caspar, and the partnering here differs in that Mitzi, created by Laura Connor, is shown lifted and controlled by four Hungarian officers as well as by Rudolf. But MacMillan reserves his biggest emotional guns for the two *pas de deux* which chart the despairing passion of Rudolf for Maria Vetsera (Lynn Seymour). In the first of these the besotted girl visits Rudolf in his apartments

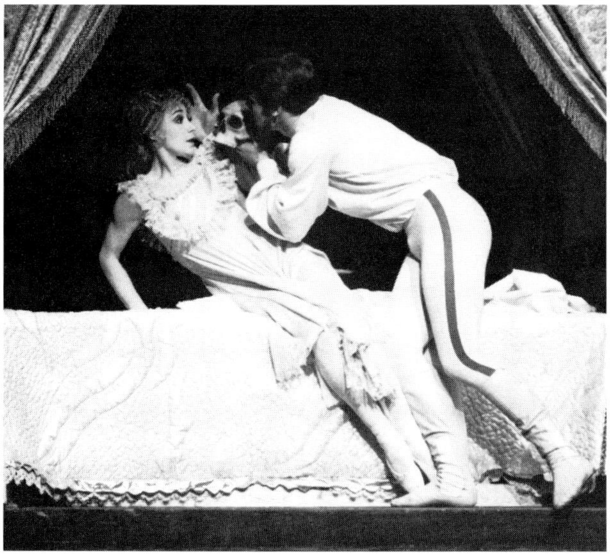

and immediately understands the fantasy world which he now inhabits. She shares his fixation with guns and with death, and it is she who provides the emotional and physical momentum for their duet – the effect is chilling and macabre. Finally, at the hunting lodge at Mayerling, Maria and Rudolf decide upon death. Rudolf is now half crazed through morphine addiction and deep rooted anguish. Their final *pas de deux* is a portrait of desperate coupling and a no less desperate awareness that death is the only solution. The *pas de deux* writing is acrobatic, its eroticism so tinctured with unhappiness that it eventually seems a cry for help. On matters of sheer practicality it demands from the male dancer resources of physical energy and of mental energy which have no precedent in ballet, all grandly evident in David Wall's interpretation of Rudolf.

There can be no greater contrast in feeling than the various duets in John Cranko's *The Taming of the Shrew* which illustrate the combative love between Katherine and Petruchio. The ballet is broad comedy, and in writing for his two stars, Marcia Haydée and Richard Cragun, Cranko was able to use both their artistic rapport – built up over many years of dancing together – and their technical bravura. In a sense Cranko was inverting this bravura since much of their double work in *Shrew* is aggressive – if Kate hacks Petruchio on the ankles, he is no less willing to knock her feet from under her and bring her crashing to the ground. Cranko was ever a master of comedy, and the sparring between the two lovers is shown to us in images that owe something to the wrestling ring, with Petruchio getting Kate in a half-nelson and Kate able to suggest that she is a nifty flyweight when the occasion presents itself. The taming of the shrew is cast throughout in comic physical terms which depend upon brilliant classical dancing and split-second timing; as a reassertion of love and order there comes a final *pas de deux*, completely serene, to seal their union, but even there Cranko cocks one last snook as Petruchio flicks Kate's nose in a gesture of huge affection and understanding.

Underlying the idea of a *pas de deux* are certain physical laws and formal rules, and the basic structure of a classical *pas de deux* illuminates these fundamental attitudes. The

Marcia Haydée as Katherine and Richard Cragun as Petruchio in one of the combative encounters in Cranko's *The Taming of the Shrew*.

Alicia Alonso and Igor Youskevitch in the Black Swan pas de deux – the firework display in the third act of *Swan Lake* – with American Ballet Theatre in Paris in 1953. This partnership, although known world-wide, was particularly celebrated in America.

pas de deux opens with an *entrée* which is in slow musical tempo and will allow the male dancer to present the ballerina and subordinate his gifts to the exhibition of her line, her balances and those qualities which are known in ballet as *adage*. This is defined in G.B.L. Wilson's admirable *Dictionary of Ballet* as: '1. A series of exercises executed to a slow tempo in the centre of the classroom to develop line and balance. 2. Name given to that part of a classical *pas de deux* in which the ballerina, supported by her partner, executes steps and achieves positions calculated to display her line and technique. The adagio is frequently the supreme moment in a classical ballet, and demands as much from the *danseur* as from the ballerina'.

This is followed by the male dancer's *variation* in which he is allowed to show off his virtuosity, and there ensures a solo variation for the ballerina. The partners are reunited for the *coda* which is traditionally in fast tempo and calls for both speed and

Marianna Tcherkassky and Fernando Bujones in the *Nutcracker* pas de deux with American Ballet Theatre at a gala in 1976. This photograph suggests the complementary nature of a partnership and reveals the qualities of turn-out and beautiful line essential in classical dancing, male and female. Bujones, trained in the School of American Ballet, is celebrated as an American danseur noble of rare distinction.

a sharing of bravura effects. For one hundred years this formal construction of the *pas de deux* has been used by choreographers from Petipa to Frederick Ashton, in such works as the third act of *Swan Lake* and the harvest scene in *La Fille mal gardée*. (This latter ballet offers a particularly engaging example of how *pas de deux* can show off the characters of the dancers who inspire it.) Petipa wrote the third act ballroom *pas de deux* in *Swan Lake* for the Italian virtuoso Pierina Legnani and interpolated into it her celebrated trick of thirty-two *fouettés* (spun turns on one toe) executed on one spot. Ashton wrote *Fille* to celebrate the buoyant charm and brilliant technique of Nadia Nerina and David Blair.

This *pas de deux* is entirely traditional since it is part of Ashton's loving reworking of an old ballet: *Fille* was first staged in Bordeaux in 1789. In the nineteenth century it gained new life in Imperial Russia where it was restaged, and Ashton paid homage to this Russian tradition when he came to make his brand new version, by incorporating mime elements and certain structural matters from the old ballet, which he learned from Tamara Karsavina, the adored Petersburg ballerina who had danced the ballet at the Maryinsky Theatre before the First World War.

Ashton wrote his *Fille* in 1960. Twelve years later Hans van Manen created a *pas de deux*, *Twilight*, for Alexandra Radius and Hann Ebbelaar of the Dutch National Ballet. This presents a duet which is strikingly different from, but also strikingly similar to, the traditional classic *pas de deux*. Instead of an orchestral score there is John Cage's *Perilous Night* for a prepared piano (pieces of wood and metal, inserted beneath the strings of the piano, produce modified timbres); instead of the traditional personalities and costuming of the two lovers – for every *pas de deux* is essentially a love duet – the boy is in a shirt and tights, the girl in a short pink dress and spikily heeled shoes. The setting is no palace or enchanted glade, but an urban industrial complex. The couple are hardly lovers in the romantic sense, but they regard each other as aggressors and the strong sexual relationship which emerges is harsh and unfeeling at the beginning. Nevertheless, the underlying structure is very much that of the classic *pas de deux* and the lovers' encounter seems brutally frank rather than sentimental.

The form of the *pas de deux*, as we have suggested, will admit of many variations, and choreographers can make duets that are funny – like MacMillan's *Sideshow* which shows a circus strong man sending up the image of masculine muscle, while a demented equestrienne tries to get her act together – or bitterly realistic, as in *Twilight*, or conventionally romantic, as we may see in the C sharp minor Waltz in *Les Sylphides*. The *pas de deux* in *Les Sylphides* for the solitary male dancer and the leading ballerina begins with an extraordinary image in that, with all the preparations for a lift having taken place in the wings, the audience sees the ballerina descending on to the stage in the dancer's arms to the first sweeping phrase of the Chopin Waltz.

It is an essentially romantic image – Mikhail Fokine created this ballet in 1908 with the deliberate intention of getting away from the rigid brilliance and constraining physical formulae of the Petipa ballets. He was looking back across Petipa to an earlier age, and in the gentleness and aspirations of romanticism he saw a way of breaking with the

Alexandra Radius and Hann Ebbelaar of the Dutch National Ballet in *Twilight*, created for them by Hans van Manen.

Peter Schaufuss as the Strong Man and Elisabetta Terabust as the Equestrienne in Kenneth MacMillan's *Side Show* which burlesques the conventions of classical ballet and of the circus.

Peter Schaufuss and Elisabetta Terabust in *Sphinx* by Glen Tetley.

The two Kirov stars Natalia Makarova and Mikhail Baryshnikov are seen in two differing partnership poses in nineteenth-century ballets. Above, the hero Solor is holding the ghost of the temple dancer Nikiya in the celebrated Shades scene from *La Bayadère*, as staged for American Ballet Theatre by Makarova. Right, the two artists are about to embark upon the mock Spanish bravura of the *Don Quixote* pas de deux.

too 'classical' present. So his *Les Sylphides* is a homage to Romanticism and the view of woman as a drifting, airy creature.

In order to achieve this impression Fokine modernised the way in which the male carried the woman in a lift. In the Waltz *pas de deux* the ballerina appears high in the air as if drifting on to the stage from the wings – she is carried in at the full extent of her partner's arms, and the effect is as if she were floating down weightlessly and of her own volition. From this moment, the developing of ballet partnering in this century has shown an increasingly arduous and sometimes acrobatic manner of manipulating the woman. The male dancer is now called upon to carry the ballerina high in the air or at arm's length – in the closing moment of the Ashton *Fille* pas de deux, after all the demands already made upon him, the hero must hold his beloved in a high one-arm lift which seems a triumphant affirmation of their happiness.

Although Ashton had used this sort of lift previously – it is to be seen in his *Sylvia* – such physical extremes were rare indeed in Western ballet until 1956 and the first London appearance of the Moscow Bolshoi Ballet. In Soviet ballets the woman held ecstatically high in a man's arms was an image which spoke clearly of the physical expansiveness and bravura which is a characteristic of post-Revolutionary Russian Ballet. In the 1920s there was much discussion and experimentation about the nature of ballet itself in the new Socialist society. In an attempt to 'democratise' what had been thought an aristocratic art, many new influences were suggested to try and broaden ballet's physical attraction for the public. The Soviet choreographer Fyodor Lopukhov did much to introduce acrobatics into ballet and his favourite ballerina, Olga Mungalova, had an astoundingly supple and sinuous body which invited many innovations in the way of showing off feminine physique. With the heroic themes that concerned Soviet ballet there also came the need for braver and more adventurous physical symbols to express them, and gradually high lifts in which the man carried the woman at arm's length or caught her in flying leaps – all of these attitudes in the West were still to be considered the province of 'adagio dancers' in the music hall – were introduced into the traditional ballets and were also exploited in the new creations of the 1930s and 1940s in Moscow and Leningrad.

The obvious exhilaration of this new sort of partnering – and one of the qualities that an audience loves in double work is the sheer daring of feats of shared virtuosity – is ideally to be seen in the concert numbers with which Soviet artists made Western audiences gasp with amazement and pleasure. Two of the most celebrated are the *Moskowski Waltz* of Vasily Vainonen and Asaf Messerer's *Spring Waters*. Both these duets demand immense confidence between the partners to bring them off. *The Moskowski Waltz* has its exultant culmination when the ballerina launches herself at the man in a leap horizontal to the floor and is caught under his arm. *Spring Waters*, set to a song by Rachmaninov, finds the couple yearning and impassioned, with the ballerina finally carried off in a rushing one-arm lift above the man's head, an apt reflection of the urgency of Rachmaninov's song and the idea of the spring thaw releasing its floods over the Russian countryside.

Above, Margot Fonteyn and Michael Somes in Ashton's *Dante Sonata*, made for the Sadler's Wells Ballet in 1940. Inspired by horrors of the war and also by Flaxman's neo-classic drawings, *Dante Sonata* was a struggle between the Children of Darkness and the Children of Light whose reaching towards heaven is vividly expressed in this beautiful lift.

One of the major developments in Soviet Ballet has been the extension of the range in partnering which can verge on the acrobatic and makes exceptional demands upon the strength of the male dancer. It also produces a huge physical excitement for the audience, as can be seen in this pose (right) from a concert number danced by Nina Sorokina and Mikhail Lavrovsky.

The high Soviet lift entered British ballet via television in 1958. In that year Margaret Dale produced a celebrated *Giselle* for BBC TV, with Nadia Nerina (right) in the title role. It was an inspired move to invite the eminent Bolshoi danseur Nicolai Fadeyechev to dance Albrecht, and he encouraged Nerina to join him in the soaring high lifts which add so much to the illusion of the spirit Giselle's weightlessness in the second act. Acrobatics have been turned into art.

Below: Desmond Kelly and Galina Samsova in *Spring Waters* by Asaf Messerer of the Bolshoi Ballet, which they performed especially for *Dancer*.

A very revealing comment upon the physical and spiritual nature of partnering comes in the contribution made by Edward Villella to an issue of *Dance Perspectives* devoted to male dancing (No. 40). 'The man does not just take an object and balance it. He takes a live individual and finds where her balance is; he anticipates her blur, putting her line back into focus and making it clear. I glory in partnering. I am not negating male bravura. That's literally my bread and butter; it's what a great portion of the ballet audience wants to see but I find all kinds of movement interesting . . . . The woman actually has a greater variety of movement than the man because she uses the additional level of full *pointe*. The man has to compensate for this by being stronger in feeling and attack . . . . Some people are so concerned about a man being a secondary figure in ballet. I don't take that. My presenting the ballerina in a *pas de deux* doesn't make me subordinate. Partnering a ballerina gives me a great pleasure and I find it a very masculine thing to do. It's very masculine to hold a door for a woman or to take her elbow to help her across the street. The male dancer does the same kind of thing. We take the woman's arm and we take her waist, we lift her and present her. It's a social as well as a balletic tradition.'

Another insider's comment, and a very illuminating one, comes from Peter Martins, the Danish star and ballet master of The New York City Ballet. In the memoirs which he wrote with Robert Cornfield, *Far from Denmark* (Little, Brown; New York, 1982), discussing his partnership with Suzanne Farrell, he says:

'Suzanne and I have danced together for so long that she has learned to trust me and to know that I will be there when she will need me, and this allows her to forget about me, and to just go about her dancing. It gives her even more freedom. Other dancers will need the security of knowing my presence all the time, and indeed it is the lively, active feel of the partner's presence that reassures them. All this changes from dancer to dancer, and it also depends on the dancer's condition. A dancer will tell you what she wants, and she'll tell you when you aren't giving her what she wants. Ballerinas always bitch: you can't lift worth a damn; don't hold me there; touch me; don't touch me.

'Years ago I was told by a ballerina after a raucous, badly-timed performance to pull myself together and to learn a few things, to shape up. She was tired of my incompetence and nonsense. So I told her to shut up and to tell the company director if she didn't want to dance with me. She never complained again, and I actually treasure the memory of our performances. She would direct me through them right on stage: "Touch me higher, right on the tits. Come on, don't be afraid, they aren't going to bump into you 'cause there isn't much of them anyway."

'There was another dancer who was less of a problem and less fun because she was so slight. She was too light, too like a feather. I didn't feel I was dancing with anything. The male partner needs to feel his partner's weight and opposition – it is the play of forces which gives a sense of drama. The audience needs to see dynamic interaction. (Suzanne's trust and her freedom to not worry about me *is* an interaction – it gives variety to the dancing, a way of measuring it out.) If nothing is there, then nothing happens,

and all you see are two dancers wandering about the stage, not as if they seem to be wishing the other would go away, but as if they didn't know the other was there at all.

'A dancer of the same weight and height as the slight one gave me a different problem. The weightlessness of the almost invisible one came from her *over*-participation (helping with a jump in a lift), but this one just placed herself and let me do all the lifting, with no help at all. Dancing with this pint-sized ballerina was like dancing with a truck. A heavy dancer is a heavy dancer, but a big one can be as light for a partner as anyone else, if she dances light and with participation.'

Partnering in the theatre is a heightened and refined reflection of attitudes which originated in social dance, as it is also in the theatre symbolic of a love affair between characters interpreted by the ballerina and her partner. Partnering in the dance theatre has always reflected the social dance manners of its time. The differing ways in which men and women have held each other in social dance reflect a matter of increasing proximity, from the courtesies of the Renaissance dance to that highly significant moment when the man's arm encircled the woman's waist in the waltz. With this closer contact there came, at the beginning of the nineteenth century, an outcry against the moral laxity which this was thought to presage, but the contact had been made and 'together dancing' became an established part of social behaviour as it also was of balletic manners.

'Together dancing', despite the occasional craze dances such as Rock 'n' Roll or Twist when the dancers rejected all contact, has remained the social norm. The great social dance partnerships, from Vernon and Irene Castle in the years immediately preceding the First World War, through the 'cheek to cheek' era of Fred Astaire and Ginger Rogers, to the ballroom dance champions of today such as the elegant Bill and Bobbie Irvine, all offer exactly the same image of two bodies thinking and moving as one. In this they are no different from the great ballet partnerships of our time – Sibley and Dowell, Haydée and Cragun, Maximova and Vasiliev.

Two aspects of partnership in the Balanchine repertory of New York City Ballet. Above, Peter Martins is seen supporting Suzanne Farrell in Balanchine's *Diamonds*, which is an evocation of the world of the classic Petipa ballet (and forms the third section of *Jewels*). Opposite page, Suzanne Farrell is being lifted by Jacques d'Amboise in *Movements*, in which Stravinksy's music and Balanchine's developed classic language form an extraordinary union.

On either side of the First World War, and during it, ballroom dancing flourished. Right, the celebrated teacher Belle Harding and her partner are dancing the 'Chic' or 'Society' Tango at the Hotel Cecil in London at a tea-dance. Below, Frank and Marguerite Gill, in evening dress, are involved in the intricacies of the Texas Rag at the Criterion in January 1914.

Two ways and two reasons to hold your partner; Marguerite and Frank Gill perform a tango, and . . .

. . . a couple stagger through the final agonies of a dance marathon in New York in the early 1930s.

Right: Santos Casani and Jose Lennard are seen in 1927 demonstrating the 'wrong' way of Charlestoning. The Charleston of the 1920s was the most frantic of the social dances of the post-war years and it led to considerable vulgarity of behaviour from men and women – hence the mysterious letters PCQ (Please Charleston Quietly) which appeared on ballroom walls. Santos Casani, a most elegant exponent of social dancing, was also a superb publicist for dancing, notably on radio in the 1930s through broadcasts and instruction programmes of dance music. On one occasion Casani and Jose Lennard danced a correct Charleston on the top of a taxi as it progressed down London's Regent Street. It made headlines.

The Jitterbug emerged during the 1930s, and soon became a craze in which the couple indulged in frankly exhibitionist and often sexually explicit gyrations that called for great physical energy and sometimes alarming display. By 1940, as we see below, the man's strength was called upon to support his partner in acrobatic holds.

Above: A wartime dance in London shows how Jitterbug fever had spread, following in the wake of the US Army.

The change in social dancing after the Second World War was gradual, but radical. Right, members of a Cardiff Dock area community are seen dancing in a exhibition of freestyle dance reminiscent of Jitterbug. Below, Jive, a development from Jitterbug, retained an extreme physicality in the 1960s as this picture of George Leslie and Anne McShane shows during the Top Rank Jive Championships of 1962. Below right, the arrival of Rock'n' Roll brought a more extravagant style of dancing.

Above: By the 1960s the Twist had arrived, with its extravagant movement and the very significant break up of the couple in dancing.
Left: With Disco in the 1970s and 1980s men and boys were dancing completely apart from their 'partners'.

The very latest dance cults emanating from New York are, left and right, Breaking, and below, Slamming. Both call for an astounding display of near-acrobatic skill and huge physical energy. Breaking is a form of street dance which emerged among the young blacks in New York, who suddenly burst into seemingly spontaneous exhibitions of spins, leaps and somersaults. Inevitably its initial raw power is being tamed for theatrical and social purposes, but it remains an entirely dazzling and highly daring activity. The young performers spin on their heads and shoulders and their gyrations are given such evocative titles as 'suicide spin' and 'moon walk'. Slamming is a dance form which has evolved in young people's clubs, and it contains elements of Hell's Angels' brutality and Punk agression. It is fiercely muscular and has a 'wall of death' bravado as the young dancers fly, boots first, into the mêlée of the Slam.

A totally different image of the male dancer from that of energetic teenager is provided by the male dancer who still remains the dominant figure in competition ballroom dancing. Ballroom dancing championships date from the 1920s and their popularity today is world-wide. The photograph above shows the elegance of style achieved by Charles Thiebault and Doreen Beahan, one of the leading couples in the 1940s. Above right, shows the technical brilliance achieved in competition or exhibition Quickstep by Richard and Janet Gleave in 1980. Right, is another form of competition and club dancing, Old Time, enjoyed especially by the middle-aged and elderly.

That the attitudes as well as the music of popular social dance can be adapted and extended in the theatre is to be seen in two famous and very different dance works: Frederick Ashton's *Façade* of 1931 and Twyla Tharp's *Baker's Dozen* of 1979. *Façade* was inspired by the social and music-hall dances of the 1920s, and it culminates in a merry burlesque of the Tango. *Baker's Dozen* is about Ragtime rethought and revitalised by a brilliant theatrical intelligence for today. It is a Tango tea for twelve white-clad dancers – they are like the wild and happy guests at one of the Great Gatsby's parties – but it calls for partnering of the greatest skill, as the bodies fly in and out of each other's arms with hair's-breadth timing. It is typical of the new demands on partnering that are much associated with Twyla Tharp's work. As a choreographer she has looked back to the social dance past of this century and by making its dance manners faster, slicker and infinitely more daring, she has created a new choreographic style of extreme bravura which relies upon exceptional trust as well as exceptional skill in partnering.

Rose Marie Wright flying in the arms of Tom Rawe and John Malashok : a characteristic moment from Twyla Tharp's *Baker's Dozen*.

Above: Anthony Dowell as the Dago and Natalia Makarova as the Débutante in Ashton's *Façade*. The role of the Dago was created by Ashton himself, but generations of English dancers have enjoyed themselves displaying its practised charm.

Right: Roland Petit rehearsing Richard Cragun in the role of Quasimodo in Petit's *Notre Dame de Paris*.

A Mutual Dependence: Dancer and Choreographer

The accomplished dancer is an artificial being, an instrument of precision, and he is forced to undergo rigorous daily exercise to avoid lapsing into his original, purely human state. His whole being becomes imbued with that same unity, that same conformity with its ultimate aim that constitutes the arresting beauty of a finished aeroplane, where every detail, as well as the general effect, expresses one supreme object – that of speed. But where the aeroplane is conceived in a utilitarian sense – the idea of beauty happening to superimpose itself upon it – the constant transfiguration, as you might call it, of the classic dancer from the ordinary to the ideal is the result of a disinterested will for perfection, an unquenchable thirst to surpass himself. Thus it is that an exalted aim transforms his mechanical effort into an aesthetic phenomenon. You may ask whether I am suggesting that the dancer is a machine? Most certainly – a machine for manufacturing beauty – if it is any way possible to conceive of a machine that in itself is a living, breathing thing, susceptible of the most exquisite emotions.

André Levinson, Theatre Arts Anthology, 1950

The relationship between a choreographer and a dancer is one of mutual dependence and mutual exploration. The choreographer depends upon the dancer as the sculptor depends upon clay or marble; and, just as the latter seeks to find qualities in those raw materials which will contribute to the work of art of which he dreams, so does the choreographer seek in the dancer possibilities and images to give life to his movement ideas. More, the dancer depends entirely upon the choreographer to give him any sort of artistic life. It is not sufficient for a dancer to be well trained in the mechanics of his art; the basic vocabulary of movement of which he is master has then to be turned in to a poetic or dramatic language by the choreographer. The dancer's identity is no more, initially, than a blank sheet of paper on which the choreographer will write, or the block of wood whose beauties of grain and texture can only be revealed in the polishing and shaping by a craftsman. The dancer will have abilities unknown to him – he does not have the gift to see himself as others see him, despite the fact that he watches his body every day in the mirrors in the studio – and it is the nature of a fine choreographer to discern abilities and talents within a dancer, and then seek to reveal them both to the dancer and to the world.

The shaping of a dancer's talent – if he has talent at all – begins in the school, and it is one of the functions of a great teacher to discern a first identity for his pupil, and to suggest ways in which that identity must be sharpened and made more physically and theatrically potent. Mikhail Baryshnikov, in his *Baryshnikov at Work*, speaks with rare perception about this matter in discussing his relationship with Alexander Pushkin. 'He often began by helping a dancer choose a line to pursue. That is, early on in his students' careers he would steer them in one direction or another: this one toward the romantic-lyrical route, that one toward the virtuoso. He taught in such a way that the dancer began to know himself more completely, and that, I believe, is the first key to serious work, to becoming an artist – to know oneself, one's gifts, one's limitations, as fully as possible. It is the only way. Any dancer will always be his own sternest critic. but real work means knowing how to invest the time, first to see yourself clearly for what you are, and then to recognise what you might become.'

But it is the greater task of a choreographer to develop these first signs of talent, to work in sympathy with the dancer's natural gifts, and also to discover certain other abilities of which the dancer may not yet be aware. This feeling for the latent power within the dancer's body and temperament does not come easily or quickly, and a choreographer needs to study his material, to watch dancers in performances and class, and to learn to 'read' their bodies before making any decisions. For, ultimately, on the choreographer's decisions depend the success or failure of the dancer as an artist. It is a commonplace of ballet that good choreography always enhances its interpreters. It is no less true that bad choreography diminishes their talents and shrinks their identity; many a bright young dancer has made a first success in a created role which has illuminated his gifts, and then has subsequently seemed disappointing and no longer talented because of the paucity of suitable choreography.

Inevitably, the identity of the male dancer has been dictated also by the social history of his time and by the very identity of man in society. We have no records, alas, of eighteenth century choreography, other than in the iconography of the period or in the notations to be found in dance manuals, but at a time when the image of the noble performer was still very strong in the theatre, when gentlemen were expected to be accomplished dancers and the female performer was still constrained by complexities of dress, there can be no doubt that male theatrical dancing was both virile and dominant.

In the ballets of Jean-Georges Noverre, an eminent choreographer of the latter part of the eighteenth century, there is no question as to the importance of the male role in the composition of his theatre works. The ballets which Noverre staged in Stuttgart, Vienna and Paris dealt with subjects, often chosen from classical mythology, of the highest seriousness and in his librettos for works such as *Agamemnon Avenged*, or *Iphigenia in Tauris*, we can deduce the challenges offered to the male dancer.

But with Romanticism this tradition of seriousness in presenting the male dancer – which had continued into the 1820s – was to be eroded by the emergence of the ballerina as the central figure in ballet, and its justification. It is not our brief to explain the many strands which brought Romanticism into the dance theatre, but we must suggest that there are certain contributory factors in the decline of the male dancer which have to do with the rise of a dominant middle class in post-Napoleonic society, and in the loss of the aristocrat as the social model for the male dancer. The subfusc image of the Victorian man, with his dark suits and his commercial aspirations, was very different from the aristocrat who was the model for the male dancers of the eighteenth century. The fantasy figure which was now the identity of the female dancer – whether as sylphide or houri – was a response to the Romantic age's desire for escape. The female dancer also was now identified with toe dancing, and this activity with its implicit idea of a flight from the ground, suggests how tenuous was to be ballet's contact with the reality of the earth; the invasion of the air, which was one of the qualities of Romanticism, was also the invasion of a world of dreams, and because Romanticism was more eager to fantasise about women the decline in male dancing began.

The arrival of the ballerina was also a response to the increasing demands made by technique and by the increasing opportunities offered the female performer. Having shed her eighteenth-century dress and been revealed in the freer, simpler lines of early nineteenth-century costume, the female body was ready to accept the technical opportunities now being proposed by such pedagogues as Carlo Blasis. Blasis's dance manual *The Code of Terpischore* indicates how clear were the opportunities for the female dancer to acquire more extensive technical prowess. The realisation of this prowess was the expansion of feminine technique typified by Maria Taglioni and Fanny Elssler. Taglioni set a fashion and incarnated a mood. With her the ballerina took the centre of the stage and the male dancer thereafter was to assume his new and subordinate position as her cavalier and supporter, the dreamer whose dream the ballerina was. His task was to carry her, to increase the illusion of lightness physically, and to provide the emotional justification for her airiness and her caprices. One of the chief commentators on the Romantic ballet, Théophile Gautier, could observe that a male dancer was 'something monstrous and indecent of which we cannot conceive'. (How different a century earlier when Voltaire praised La Camargo, most brilliant dancer of her time, by saying that 'she danced like a man'.)

Maria Taglioni's father was the choreographer Filippo Taglioni, and we can infer from the details of her career how much time he devoted to promoting her art in the ballets which he staged for her. There was little place in these works for any male dancer as rival; his position was merely to set off the divinity's charm and lightness. The banishing of the male dancer was to be a gradual process, but it is noteworthy that Maria Taglioni herself was unwilling to share the limelight with her partner. Between 1830 and 1835 she was partnered by Jules Perrot, an outstanding male virtuoso. His excellence was such that a critic would write, 'One forgets that he is a male dancer.' Taglioni herself could not forget this fact, and Perrot's success at her side prompted the outburst: 'Is it not terrible when a male dancer is given more applause than I am? It is infamous.' Maria Taglioni's view of her own importance in her father's ballets was once acutely noted by another critic, who observed that 'all Father Taglioni's ballets are alike: a complete absence of ideas, secondhand stuff, always the same . . . but the ballerina is there to rescue the choreographer, the daughter to rescue the father.' Typical of Filippo Taglioni's ability to provide the public with the balletic feminism now in fashion was his *La Révolte au Sérail* in which the women in a harem rebel and are shown as an Amazon army.

Maria Taglioni's contemporary, Fanny Elssler, with her passionate acting and that sensuality which won the heart of every man in the audience, was sometimes seen partnered by her taller, elder sister Thérèse, an event which provoked nothing but admiring comments on the charm of Thérèse, and may be seen as a forerunner of the later reliance upon pretty girls wearing breeches in *travesti* roles.

That male dancing continued at all to be of any theatrical significance we must attribute to the gifts of a few male dancers as choreographers. Jules Perrot was forced to leave the Paris Opéra in 1835 when he was at the height of his powers as a dancer. Thereafter he took an itinerant route through Europe dancing and staging ballets and in Naples met and fell in love with the enchantingly pretty Italian dancer Carlotta Grisi. He educated her and in her developing abilities saw a means of returning to the centre of the ballet stage in Paris as her partner and choreographer. In this he was only partially successful. He launched Carlotta's career, and in 1841 saw her triumph in *Giselle*, for whose choreography he was in part responsible. But his greatest achievements lay ahead. In 1842 he came to London and there began a period of very important creativity as choreographer. In the ballets which he staged at Her Majesty's Theatre – *Ondine* 1843, *La Esmeralda* 1844, *Eoline* 1845, *Caterina* and *Lalla Rookh* 1846 – he showed works more serious and more interesting in the presentation of the male dancer than any of the extravaganzas produced at the Paris Opéra. Ivor Guest in his invaluable *Romantic Ballet in London* speaks of Perrot's 'great sympathy with humanity, which showed itself in the delineation of his characters. These were never cardboard figures. Often, his heroes were not conventional princes or nobles, but men of quite humble origin – Matteo, the fisherman in *Ondine* for example and Pierre Gringoire, the itinerant poet in *La Esmeralda* . . . .'

Even though Perrot was able to maintain some interest and dignity in his male characters, he had nevertheless to succumb to the ballerina-mania of the time. He staged a *pas de deux* in 1843 which featured Fanny Elssler and Fanny Cerrito, darlings of the public, and two years later produced one of the best remembered works of this era, the *Pas de Quatre* which brought together four of the chief ballerinas of the age, Taglioni, Cerrito, Grisi and Grahn. In the following year came *The Judgement of Paris* for Taglioni, Cerrito and Grahn, with Perrot and his colleague Arthur St Léon in minor roles; in 1847 *Les Eléments* for Cerrito, Grisi and Carolina Rosati; and finally in 1848 *The Four Seasons*, which starred Cerrito, Grisi, Rosati and the young Maria Taglioni (the greater Marie's niece).

It is works like these – St Léon called them steeplechases – that we see how in the declining years of Romanticism the male dancer was of no importance in the public eye. Happily, Perrot was to find a post for the decade from 1849 onwards in St Petersburg, as first ballet master, and it was here that he could restage many of his major works and help build the greatness of the Imperial Russian Ballet.

Perrot's colleague St Léon had started life as a child prodigy, as both dancer and violinist. He was an unquestionably brilliant dancer, and he sustained the importance of male dancing at a time when it was beginning to go into eclipse. He married the dancer Fanny Cerrito, and appeared with her in ballets in which he both danced and choreographed and played the violin, and it is some comment on his importance that Gautier could write:

'St Léon was also well received; which reminds us that not for a long time has a genuine male dancer been seen in France; the marked disfavour into which male dancing had fallen having very considerably reduced the choreographic portion in ballets that

Left: Malvina Cavallazzi was an Italian ballerina who appeared in London between 1887 and 1899, specialising in travesty roles at the Empire Theatre. This costume design by Wilhelm shows her as Edmond Dantès in *Monte Cristo*. She is about as credible a hero as the ballet was an interpretation of the Dumas novel.

Right: Arthur St Léon (1821–1870) as he appears in his own ballet *Le Lutin de la Vallée* at the Théâtre Lyrique in Paris in 1853. Dancer, choreographer, violinist, briefly husband of Fanny Cerrito, St Léon was an extraordinary virtuoso, one of the last to persuade the public of the validity of male dancing by the force of his personality and the very evident power of his technique.

is allotted to men. Lucien Petipa himself, a charming actor, an expressive and passionate mime, seemed to be asking forgiveness for his dancing, and for his acting, by devoting himself exclusively to setting off the graces of his partner. Since Perrot's retirement St Léon is the only one who dared to dance at the Opéra for the sake of dancing, and all have been surprised at his success.'

Yet for the real importance of male dancing and for both its moral and physical dignity we have to turn to Jules Perrot's contemporary, Auguste Bournonville. Born in Copenhagen in 1805, the son of French dancer Antoine Bournonville and his Swedish wife, Auguste throughout his life was proudly Danish. He was destined to be a dancer – many dancers male and female in the eighteenth and nineteenth centuries followed a family tradition of working in the theatre – and was to gain his first comprehension of the possibilities of male dancing when his father took him to Paris as a boy of fifteen to work with Auguste Vestris. The effect on young Auguste was profound. He returned to Copenhagen after this amazing summer, but three years later, when his father had been dismissed from the Royal Theatre, Copenhagen, as ballet director, the young Auguste realised that if he was to achieve anything as a dancer he must return to Paris, and in April 1824 he arrived there for two years' study. His *Memoirs* and his letters home reveal how hard he worked with Vestris, absorbing from this master everything of the French style of dancing at its best. After two years he was accepted into the ballet of the Paris Opéra, and there came the difficult task of breaking his implicit contract with the Royal Danish Ballet and remaining as an increasingly important member of the Paris Opéra Ballet. Nevertheless, he knew that he must go back to Copenhagen; his heart was there and he sensed that it was incumbent upon him to attempt to revive the moribund Danish ballet. Thus he took leave from the Paris Opéra, returned to Copenhagen where the King granted him permission to perform, and in the autumn of 1829 astounded the Danish public by his grace and expressive force.

The result was forgiveness for his unscheduled years away, and an initial contract – for the astounding period of no fewer than eighteen years – as principal dancer, choreographer, leader of the ballet and court dancing master. Bournonville's task was clear – to rebuild the fortunes of the Royal Danish Ballet – and fortunately his abilities were more than adequate for this task. Despite brief periods when he worked in Vienna and Stockholm, the next forty-seven years show us Bournonville creating dances and dancers, and imposing a view of ballet and of the dancer's identity upon Danish society which sought for both moral and physical harmony. Informing everything he did was Bournonville's belief in the dignity and beauty of dancing as an art, and in the honourable state of dancing as a career. In staging ballets, Bournonville was guided not only by his abhorrence of the excesses of Romanticism, but also by an understandable pride in his own gifts. Thus, nowhere in his ballets do we find the sickly imbalance which had elsewhere in Europe reduced the male dancer to the ignominious position of fetcher and carrier of the ballerina. The heroes in Bournonville's ballets are virile, their behaviour is expressed in vivid and demanding dance terms, their relationship with women, though sometimes idealised, is recognisably human rather than couched in the stereotyped terms of the French ballet. There is a mutual respect between men and women in many of Bournonville's works which reflects his concern for society's respect for dancers.

It is ironic that the Bournonville ballet which is most widely known in the world today is the least characteristic in its moral attitudes. Bournonville staged *La Sylphide* after Taglioni's Paris original because he wished to present his pupil Lucile Grahn in the image of Maria Taglioni. He refused to make the role of James as subordinate as it had been in the Paris production, but nevertheless he could not escape the uneasy emotional resolution of Filippo Taglioni's ballet, and thus we have the (for Bournonville) 'uncharacteristic' ending showing the hero James eventually destroyed by passion and by evil, whereas in every other dramatic work Bournonville asserts the triumph of virtue and of decent feeling.

Rarely, in the nineteenth-century ballets surviving today, do we see as clearly as with Bournonville the inspiration behind the role. The outward appearance of Bournonville dancing for men is soaring, bold, light and life-embracing. There is an openness, a joyous assurance of temperament, which is exactly reflected in the brilliant and tireless physical

These figures from Elith Reumert's *History of the Danish Ballet*, published in Copenhagen in 1922, illustrate the vital tradition of Danish male dancing in two major Bournonville ballets: Left, the ardent hero of *La Ventana* and right, Gennaro in *Napoli*. It is interesting to note that type of costuming has remained constant almost to today – Gennaro's Neapolitan outfit is almost sacrosanct.

outlines of the dance. The eminent Danish critic and historian Erik Aschengreen, writing in the programme for the centenary celebrations of Bournonville's death in 1979, observed: 'When the Royal Danish Ballet was really discovered by international criticism and the international public after the Second World War, it was precisely the male dancers who surprised. A number of things which had disappeared or had been neglected in the rest of Europe were still being cultivated in Denmark. This had to do primarily with the ability of the men to leap, their elevation and *ballon*. These technical skills were demanded by Bournonville's choreography and were therefore part of the daily training in the ballet school where the two great ballet masters following Bournonville, Hans Beck and Harald Lander, were both aware of the unique value of the Bournonville tradition.

'The Danish male dancers became strong, light and free, but it is important to add that technique was never a goal in itself for Bournonville. He knew from his days as a dancer that desire to dazzle the audience with technical virtuosity and to bring down the house with bravura dancing, but he fought against this tendency in himself and in others. Dance was not only steps and technique. Art was to be used in the service of higher things, and Bournonville was not satisfied with developing the technical possibili-

Right: Hans Beck and Valborg Borchsenius in Bournonville's *Napoli*. Bournonville died in 1879 and shortly before his death he saw the debut of the young Hans Beck. Beck did not die until 1952, at the age of 91, and it was he who lovingly preserved and edited the Bournonville repertory and style in Copenhagen.

ties of the body and even less interested in sensuality. Art had to do with the spirit for Bournonville. Art was to be used to elevate and liberate the mind. The ballets of Bournonville deal with people and with their relationships both to this world and to what lies beyond it . . .

'In Bournonville ballets such as *Napoli*, *A Folk Tale*, and *La Sylphide*, the men are literally the central characters and a Bournonville dancer must, in addition to technical proficiency, have talent for mime and plastic expression . . .

'Bournonville's heroes are not just masculine, high-flying, elegant jumpers. They are also sensitive young men with inner problems. It is perhaps here that we may find the underlying reasons why great dancers are so interested in working on these characters, just as the rich humanity of these figures may be the reason that we the audience never become tired of seeing these ballets. Every new artist dances Bournonville's steps but he interprets the ballet according to his own temperament. When an artist understands how to approach the role from the inside and lets Bournonville's choreography meet his own mind, these romantic youths become living and important to us. It is the inheritance Bournonville left the Danish, and the international male dancer, a legacy that is still a challenge and that yields rich, rich rewards.'

Above: A scene from Bournonville's *A Folk Tale*. The ballet concerns the beautiful Hilda (Mette Ida Kirk, centre) who has been stolen by the Trolls when a baby. Her foster mother Muri (Lillian Jensen) stands behind and the Troll brothers Viderik and Diderik (Niels Kehlet and Fredbjørn Bjørnsson) are quarrelling over who shall marry Hilda. The Troll scenes in this ballet depend upon the wonderful ability of the Danish artist to play mime roles, and it is significant that Kehlet and Bjørnsson, both great classic danseurs in the Bournonville repertory in their time, have now moved on to playing character roles such as these with no less bravura.

Right: The importance of the male dancer in the Bournonville repertory is clearly evident in *Kermesse in Bruges*, whose story hinges on the adventures of three brothers, danced here by Poul Vessel, Fredbjørn Bjørnsson and Svend Erik Jensen.

Erik Bruhn was generally acknowledged as the embodiment of the most refined and elegant style in post-war ballet in the West. Trained in the Royal Danish Ballet School, he moved into the larger world of ballet and conquered every audience by his impeccable dancing. Above, he is James in the second act of *La Sylphide*; right, he is seen in a solo from *The Nutcracker*.

Because Copenhagen was not considered in the early years of this century to be in the main stream of European ballet the quality of Bournonville's choreography, and the tradition of male excellence both in virtuoso and character roles, was largely unknown. Certain outstanding Danish dancers, notably Erik Bruhn, had been seen from 1947 onwards in London and Paris, but it was not until the Royal Danish Ballet plucked up courage to stage annual festivals in its home theatre, and then to venture out into the wider world, that the glories of Danish male dancing and of Bournonville's choreography were to win the affections of the international ballet public.

It is from the Covent Garden season in 1954 that we would date the general recognition of the Danish *danseur* as an artist supremely elegant and gifted. Thenceforward, Bournonville training became synonymous with excellence for men. We have already mentioned the prodigious impact of Erik Bruhn; other virtuosos – Fredbjørn Bjørnsson, Frank Schaufuss, Flemming Flindt, Henning Kronstam, Niels Kehlet, Flemming Ryberg, Peter Martins, Peter Schaufuss, Arne Villumsen, Ib Andersen among them – subsequently enjoyed as much fame outside Denmark as on their native stage. It is to certain of these artists also that we owe the spread of Bournonville choreography into the international repertory, where it provides both a joy and a challenge for dancers. Today, most self-respecting ballet companies own one or more Bournonville works, and Peter Schaufuss has been notably successful in reviving the masterworks that are part of his inheritance: his version of *La Sylphide* for London Festival Ballet, for the Stuttgart Ballet and for Roland Petit's Ballet de Marseille; his *Napoli* for the National Ballet of Canada, and his *A Folk Tale* for the Ballet of the Deutsche Oper in West Berlin, have all shown how these nineteenth-century jewels can be reset for new generations of dancers and for new audiences, with intelligence and profound sympathy.

Niels Kehlet and Solveig Østergaard in the first act of Bournonville's *Napoli*. In this buoyant Bournonville jump we can see both the joyous spring of Danish style and that sense of companionship which is so vital in the relationship between the hero and heroine in these old ballets.

Flemming Flindt in *La Ventana* by Bournonville. Here is another aspect of the Bournonville male dancer's joyous command of the air. Flindt, a most distinguished dancer, was for several years director of the Royal Danish Ballet and has choreographed for stage and television.

Linda Hindberg and Flemming Ryberg in the last act divertissement from *Napoli* as presented by the Royal Danish Ballet at the Royal Theatre in Copenhagen in the Bournonville centenary celebrations of 1979. The freedom of the Bournonville style is here apparent. Flemming Ryberg is one of the purest exponents of Bournonville dancing, a celebrated James in *La Sylphide*.

On the bridge that forms part of the set of the last act of *Napoli* children from the school of the Royal Danish Ballet traditionally make their first appearance on stage, watching, learning and cheering as the cascade of dances pours over the stage. This artistic continuity is one of the great strengths of the Danish company.

Right: Peter Martins and two fellow matelots in Balanchine's *Union Jack* staged for New York City Ballet as part of the company's Bicentennial celebrations. One of the outstanding Danish dancers of his generation, Martins joined New York City Ballet as a guest artist in 1968 and was appointed a principal in the following year. His heroic appearance and technique won him many central roles in the Balanchine repertory, and eventually he was appointed chief ballet master of NYCB jointly with Jerome Robbins. Balanchine's admiration for Bournonville schooling has meant that both Danish teaching (in the person of the eminent teacher Stanley Williams) and Danish dancing, through such artists as Peter Martins and Ib Andersen, have become increasingly important with NYCB.

Below: Peter Martins and Suzanne Farrell in *Bournonville Divertissement* as staged for New York City Ballet. The grandeur and distinction of Martins's dancing which has brought so much to the Balanchine repertory is obvious in this picture of him dancing in the *Flower Festival in Genzano* pas de deux.

Arne Villumsen, a leading dancer of the Royal Danish Ballet, in *Napoli*. In its expansiveness and sense of freedom, as well as its classic exactness, this picture tells everything of the essential qualities of Bournonville schooling.

Suzanne Farrell and Ib Andersen in Balanchine's *Mozartiana*. The New York City Ballet's Danish connection was strengthened still further by the arrival of the young Danish star Ib Andersen in 1979. In his native Bournonville repertory Ib Andersen was an exceptional exponent of the best qualities of Bournonville schooling, and after his arrival in New York he quickly assumed many of the leading roles in the Balanchine repertory. In *Mozartiana* of 1981 Balanchine choreographed a dazzling role for Ib Andersen to set against his portrait of Suzanne Farrell as the central figure in what was his fourth version of this Tchaikovsky homage to Mozart.

Although the male dancer retained a highly positive image as performer in Copenhagen, elsewhere in Europe, as we have suggested, his position was invidious. In France men were called upon to perform character roles of minor importance at the Opéra, and a few principal roles were reserved for them, but the casting of a pretty girl as the hero of *Coppélia* in 1870 and of *Les Deux Pigeons* in 1886 is indicative of public taste and public contempt for the man as dancer. In England ballet had been banished to the music hall, and the dance entertainments at the Alhambra and the Empire Theatres relied upon buxom young ladies in unconvincing travesty to take such leading male roles as there might be. While the public were quite happy to watch men dancing in the robust traditions of music hall during its heyday, the more rarefied world of the ballet still believed that it was better to keep men offstage. Even as late as 1910, when the Empire Theatre put on a full-scale production of *Sylvia*, the only male dancer was Fred Farren in the grotesque role of Pan; the hero, Aminta, and Eros were taken by very pretty girls.

The picture was entirely similar in the United States. There was both a lively tradition of black minstrel dancing (which was supremely to be seen in the Cakewalk), and all forms of social dancing knew a popularity which ignored any boundaries of location and class. In the theatre, however, 'ballet' meant the kind of extravaganzas typified for us by two celebrated examples, *The Black Crook* and *The White Fawn*, which triumphed variously across America for more than twenty years.

The total decadence of French ballet at the turn of the 20th century is exemplified by this picture of the hero and heroine in *Les Deux Pigeons* at the Paris Opéra, when Carlotta Zambelli is being 'partnered' by the buxom Antonine Meunier.

Adèle Dumilâtre and Eugène Coralli in *La Gypsy*. The ballet was set in Edinburgh and involved a missing child and a troupe of gypsies. This lithograph by Deveria indicates the dramatic vigour that was still allowed a male character dancer in the Romantic ballet.

The Cakewalk originated in the finales of the Black Minstrel shows so popular at the end of the last century, and it involved a strutting progress round the stage by gorgeously dressed dancers. This eventually led to the adaptation of the Cakewalk as a social entertainment which in time entered the ballrooms of Europe. Like every other social dance it stressed the man's proud presentation of his lady. Above: 'Cake Walk' by Albert Myers (1890?).

This poster for *The Black Crook*, as staged in New York in 1866 and revived constantly thereafter, says everything about the debasement of ballet in the latter part of the nineteenth century. Curves and coyness were all.

The Black Crook opened in New York in 1866 and its advance publicity announced a 'great Parisienne ballet troupe' with a listing of thirty-one featured *danseuses* and 'fifty auxiliary ladies'. But there is no mention anywhere of the name of a male dancer, though the leading ballerina Maria Bonfanti is seen in a contemporary photograph with a gentleman decorously in attendance.

It was only in Imperial Russia that male dancing knew anything like the respect which it had in Copenhagen. We cannot pretend that the spectacular ballets staged there by Perrot and St Léon and then by Marius Petipa (who was chief ballet master from 1869–1903) did not have the ballerina as their justification, but at no time was male dancing allowed to fall into decline: in the school the traditions of an excellent training were established, and on stage the hero was called upon to be both noble and virile, while character performances were thought to be of real importance in the framework of the ballet.

Perhaps the most interesting testimony concerning the identity of the male dancer and his relationship with the choreographer comes in the Memoirs of Nicholas Legat. Born in 1869, a member of one of those dynastic dance families which contributed so much to the perpetuation of the traditions of male dancing in Russia as in Denmark, Legat graduated in to the ballet at the Maryinsky Theatre in 1888, remained as a principal dancer until 1915, and was also director of the Imperial Ballet School.

Legat was of the generation that made the great breakthrough in male dancing in Russia. His immediate predecessor was the eminently noble Pavel Gerdt, who was the first Prince in Petipa's *Sleeping Beauty* and the first Siegfried in the Petipa/Ivanov *Swan Lake* of 1895 (Gerdt was at that time already fifty-one years old). In his art Gerdt exemplified the qualities demanded by both Petipa's choreography and by the public – elegance of manner and a princely distinction of bearing. With Legat we can note the increasing insistence upon technical skill, in part inspired by the appearance in Russia of the Italian virtuoso dancers – notably Enrico Cecchetti. With Legat's heirs and successors we enter a golden age of Russian male dancing with such artists as Nijinsky, Fokine and Bolm, whose technical and artistic standards conditioned the new public image of the male dancer in the West.

Legat's entire dancing career was spent in Russia and his *The Story of the Russian School* (1932) provides unique insights into the tradition of male dancing and the training in the Imperial Ballet. The diplomatist, Sir Paul Dukes, in his introduction to Legat's book provided a vivid picture of the world in which Legat worked: 'I shall never forget a brilliant ballet evening at the Imperial Maryinsky Theatre in the month of January 1914. It was one of those occasions for which it was quite impossible for anyone but the most influential to procure tickets, but Monsieur Tartakoff, the Director of the Theatre and a good friend, relaxed so far as to allow me to stand just inside of the door of the central aisle. The audience was composed of the elite of the Russian nobility. The place blazed with jewels and uniforms. The strains of the National Anthem sounded, everyone rose, and all eyes were fixed on the Imperial box as the Tsar, the Tsarina and the Imperial family entered and took their places. The orchestra, under Richard Drigo, broke into the overture and the curtain rose on the ballet *Esmeralda*. It was a gala night but it was also more than that, it was a jubilee night. One by one the chief artists emerged to meet with warm receptions – the beautiful Matilda Kshesinskaya as Esmeralda, the dignified Paul Gerdt as Frollo, the celebrated mime Stukolkin as Quasimodo. Then about half way through the first act, a slight figure in a green jerkin, the poet Gringoire, was dragged on the stage by brigands. Suddenly the performance came to a stop. The entire auditorium rose to its feet. Even the Tsar stood. On the stage the performers deserted their positions to acclaim their colleague, who remained in the centre bowing incessantly, clearly moved to tears by this acclamation. The poet Gringoire was Nicholas Legat, and the occasion the celebration of his jubilee of 25 years service in the Imperial Theatre. The demonstration, which lasted a good fifteen minutes, and was repeated again in the next two acts, was a tribute of public admiration. In the last act, tables were brought on and piled with gifts and presents, while the hero of the day received address after address from countless organisations. One telegram read: "Terpsichore has shown her riches by giving us Legat".'

Pavel Gerdt as Prince Désiré in the first production of *The Sleeping Beauty* in 1890. At the age of 45, Gerdt was no longer a *jeune premier*, but his elegance and distinction of manner were still an outward and visible sign of his greatness as leading male dancer of the Imperial Ballet in St Petersburg.

This studio portrait shows Nicholas Legat (1869–1937) in the conventional classical costume of his time. What is quite clear is a handsome assurance and well-trained legs.

In this posed picture of Legat as Siegfried to Pavlova's Odette in *Swan Lake* we see how even a leading male dancer was concerned to display the ballerina.

The ballets which showed off the generations of Gerdt and Nicholas Legat were the creations of Marius Petipa, and this master's fifty-six years of service in Russia provide an exact view of the choreographic identity given to the male. From 1862, when Petipa staged his first success, *Pharaoh's Daughter*, in St Petersburg, his creations were to follow an inevitable formula: that of the grand spectacular ballet, generous in narrative, massive in effects, and designed to show off the ballerina as prime justification for the evening's entertainment, but nevertheless surrounding her with an exceptional richness of other dance incidents.

The identity of the male dancer as hero was, of course, preserved though his technical identity was very much beneath that of the ballerina. The prominence nowadays seized by male dancers in contemporary stagings of the old Petipa classics – *La Bayadère*, *The Sleeping Beauty* and *Swan Lake*, for example – in no way represents their original importance. It is an interesting aspect of the increasing significance of male dancing in our time that such *premiers danseurs* as Erik Bruhn, Rudolf Nureyev and Mikhail Baryshnikov have built up the amount of dancing in their productions of the 'classics' to redress what they see as an imbalance between male and female dancing.

But whatever importance Petipa and his audience knew to be necessary to honour the ballerina's presence in these old ballets, there was nevertheless an awareness that the man, as virtuoso and as character performer, needed to be considered, and an examination of the narratives of Petipa's works as we seen them in the scenarios, interestingly preserved in Cyril Beaumont's *Complete Book of Ballets*, reveals that the male contribution to the dramatic scheme was not inconsiderable.

The old ballets were of course stereotyped both in their ideas and in their performance manner. The hidebound nature of the audience in St Petersburg – largely aristocratic and, like the ballet, dependent upon the Tsar's approval – is reflected in the hidebound conventions of the ballet itself. Thus Mikhail Fokine, an eminent *danseur* before he set about trying to liberate the ballet through his own choreographies, could write in his *Memoirs* of the frustrating world of the ballet which he entered when he joined the Imperial Ballet in 1898 as an eighteen-year-old soloist:

'We, the male classic dancers did not have either the appearance or the manners required by our roles, and were limited to what was demanded by the dance – which is a very different thing; for none of our dances was part of a role, or the expression of a certain character. In fact each dance was nothing more than a demonstration of agility

Right: Anna Pavlova as the Pharaoh's daughter and Mikhail Mordin (1881–1944) as Lord Wilson in the opening scene of Petipa's *Pharaoh's Daughter* as staged in Moscow in 1905. The ballet deals with a Victorian traveller, Lord Wilson, who takes refuge in a pyramid during a sandstorm and there dreams of Egypt's great past. Mordkin and Pavlova had a stormy relationship, not least when he partnered the ballerina in her world tours – she had occasion to slap his face in public in London. A dancer of exceptional virility and power, Mordkin was not prepared merely to act as an attendant on the divinity. After a distinguished career in Russia Mordkin went to America in 1923 and performed with his own company, while students from his school were to become, in 1939, the eventual nucleus of what is now the American Ballet Theatre. Mordkin did much to promote a stronger image of male dancing in America.

and virtuosity. . . . When I played a "mime" role I represented an authentic image of the period. But when I danced a "classic" part, I portrayed a leading dancer – outside the confines of place or time, with marcelled hair, pink cheeks and ballet tights. Sometimes, in the very same role – such as that of Jean de Brienne in *Raymonda* (I was given this role after several years of service) – I appeared in the second act and in the beginning of the third as a knight crusader, attired in an historically correct costume, because there was no dancing in these scenes, only pantomime, swordplay, rescue of a lady, and so on; but in the middle of the third act I removed my wig and hastily waved my hair into sheep-like curls, thus preparing myself for my forthcoming *variation*. My colleague, Oboukhov, in the role of the troubadour Béranger in the same ballet, would hurriedly transform his hair from blond to dark.'

These two chaps were helping to give ballet a bad name. Or maybe it was the photographer – or more likely the costumier – for they are principal dancers of the Imperial Moscow Ballet at the beginning of this century. Laurent Novikov seems to think he is a butterfly, while Mikhail Mordkin is modelling ancient Egyptian beachwear.

It was against these mindless conventions that Fokine sought to rebel within the Maryinsky Theatre itself. Despite official indifference he set about making ballets – his early works in Russia include *Chopiniana* (*Les Sylphides*) and *Le Pavillon d'Armide* – in which he broke away from the hallowed manner of Petipa to a freer and more contemporary form of expression. His aspirations for a 'new ballet' in many ways corresponded with creators in the other arts who were seeking to drag music and painting away from nineteenth-century academic constraints. Thus it was that Fokine eventually was introduced to Serge Diaghilev. Diaghilev had already made a great reputation for himself as an apostle of the new in art and when, in 1909 Diaghilev organised a season of Russian opera and ballet in Paris, it was Fokine who was to provide those first choreographies which astounded the west.

That both Mordkin and Novikov were, on the contrary, important and serious artists can be seen in these two photographs which show, on the left, Mordkin as Albrecht in the first act of *Giselle* in Moscow in 1907 with Vera Karalli, and Novikov with Anna Pavlova in *Amarilla* in 1912.

Diaghilev had recruited dancers from Petersburg and Moscow to appear in this brief season. The women, led by Pavlova and Karsavina, astonished and delighted audiences, but it was the male dancing of Nijinsky and Adolph Bolm which was to be greatest revelation to Paris. Among the works presented was the Polovtsian scene from Borodin's *Prince Igor*. The setting is a Tartar camp where the fierce Polovtsian warriors dance in celebration. It is this explosion of truly virile virtuosity, led by Adolph Bolm as the chief warrior, which aroused the Parisian audience to the greatest enthusiasm and must be seen as announcing the rebirth of male dancing before a Western audience. Even the normally unemotional Serge Grigoriev, stage director for the Diaghilev Ballet throughout its existence, was moved in his *Memoirs* to say of the impression produced by the Polovtsian Dances that 'when the curtain came down the pandemonium was indescribable'.

Of course much attention in this first sight of the Russian dancers was accorded to Vaslav Nijinsky. His was a most special as well as a most prodigious gift. In St Petersburg his technical abilities had been recognised from his schooldays. Now, as a very young man and as Diaghilev's beloved, he was to have a series of roles made for him in the succeeding four years which explored his astounding power of identification with a character. He was not best seen in the conventionally princely roles; far more impressive were his impersonations of the exotic, mysterious or other-worldly beings created for him by Fokine. His first Parisian success was in two existing Fokine roles – the 'youth of the Chopin type' who is the sole male in *Les Sylphides*, and Armida's slave in *Le Pavillon d'Armide*, in which Nijinsky's role was that of extraordinary virtuoso, best revealed in a variation in which, as C. W. Beaumont noted in *The Complete Book of Ballets*, he 'crossed from one side of the stage to the other by means of a series of vertical bounds, *entrechats* and *tours en l'air*, in which he rose and fell and rose again with the softness and ease of a bounding ball'.

Subsequently Fokine set about devising those highly specialised roles which explored the range of Nijinsky's genius. First came *Scheherazade*, in which Nijinsky was the Golden Slave, dancing with a pantherine sensuality. Then came *Le Spectre de la Rose*, a duet for Nijinsky and Karsavina in which he soared into a young girl's bedroom as the incarnation of the rose that she had worn at her first ball, and had to seem both as heady and as transient as the scent of the rose itself. Next, in 1911, came the self-absorbed Narcissus of *Narcisse* and then in this same year the pathetic puppet of *Petrushka* – there could hardly be a greater contrast between the rose, or the beautiful youth of *Narcisse*, with Nijinsky's puppet who, in Beaumont's words, 'seemed to have limbs of wood and a face made of plaster, in which his eyes resembled nothing so much as two boot buttons. Only now and again did he make you aware that beneath this façade there was a tiny spark of human life, which you caught sight of by accident, as though it were something you were not meant to see. Gone were those fascinating features with the slanting eyes, that marvellous elevation. All had vanished to be replaced by this wretched puppet – beaten, humiliated, and the sport of its fellows – a victim of cruel injustice which moved by jerks and starts and hardly left the ground'.

The change in public interest in male dancing brought about by the first Diaghilev seasons is nowhere more clearly indicated than in Cocteau's famous poster showing Nijinsky as the Spirit of the Rose.

In 1912 Fokine made two more roles for Nijinsky, neither of them successful; first as the exotic Blue God marvellously dressed by Bakst in *Le Dieu Bleu*, and then as the gentle Daphnis in *Daphnis and Chloe*. But it was in this year, too, that Nijinsky made his first role for himself as the Faun in *L'Après-midi d'un faune*. This we must see as the first modern choreography of the twentieth century. But once again the role was other-worldly – in this case both mythic and animal – and in this, as in Nijinsky's next choreography, for *Jeux* in 1913, he is still seen as being very different from the ordinary run of mankind. In *Jeux* (which Diaghilev thought of as a work of the future, saying 'we date it 1930') Nijinsky's role was the new sporting image of man in a ballet whose ostensible concern with tennis was a mask for flirtation. No film remains to show anything of Nijinsky's dancing. Yet the photographs taken of him, especially those by Baron de Meyer, so vividly capture his personality that we can sense a great deal about his roles and about his ability to transform himself totally from one character to the next. These photographs are superbly reproduced and analysed in Lincoln Kirstein's *Nijinsky Dancing* (Knopf 1975), and a comparison of the figure in *Scheherazade* with the Faun and the Rose will immediately convey the transformations wrought by genius.

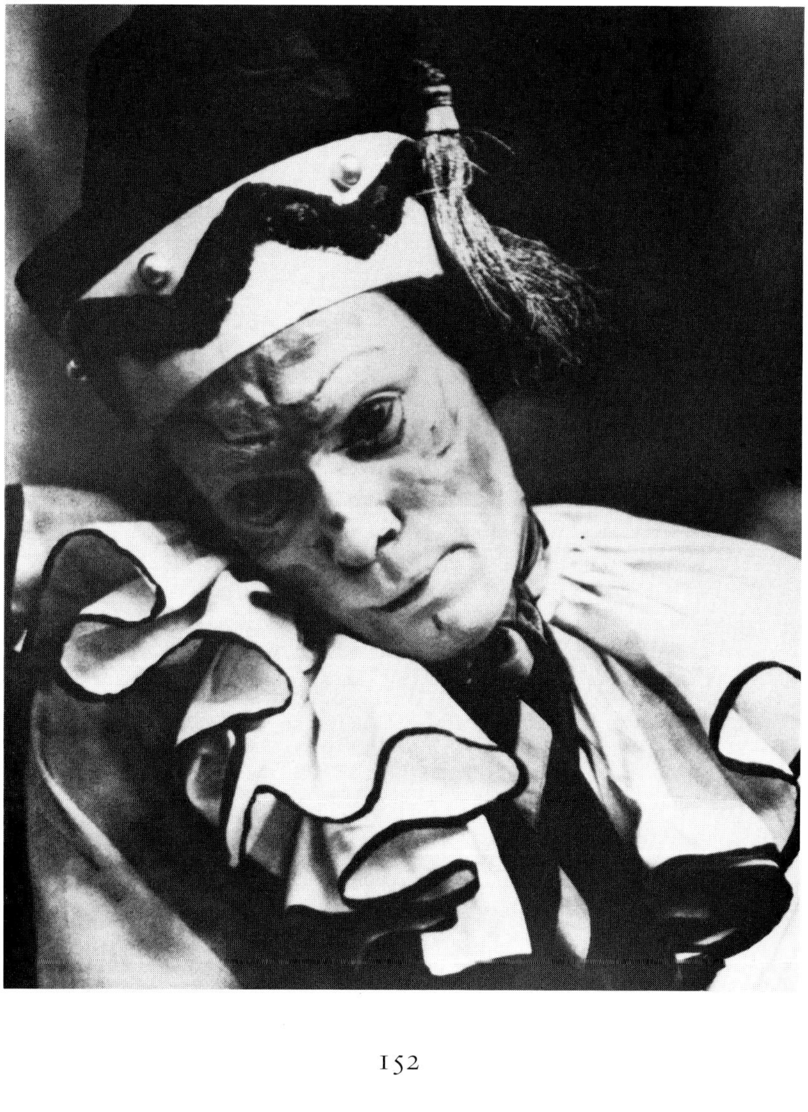

It was this genius which set him apart from the common run of male dancers. His roles, like his performances, were unique and, as with Pavlova, his name has become synonymous with dancing (a distinction shared today only by Rudolf Nureyev).

Although Diaghilev was obsessed with Nijinsky, he realised that his idol could only properly be appreciated within the context of a well-balanced company; indeed, throughout the twenty-year existence of the Diaghilev enterprise, the male dancer shared equal prominence with the women.

The magic of Nijinsky's presence and the mystery of his genius as a dance artist are very clear in these photographs. We have but to contrast the twisted, subhuman puppet Petrushka (left) with the romantic ardour of Albrecht in act II of *Giselle* (below) to see something of the transformation of which the dancer was capable on stage. In the photograph on the right he is the male dancer as a 20th-century figure in his own ballet, *Jeux*.

Left: Nijinsky is the sensual and irresistible Golden Slave in *Scheherazade*. Very different is the image projected of his faun (right), which was an animal being, while in a Georgian dance, a Lezghinka (below), he personifies the dash of Russian character dancing.

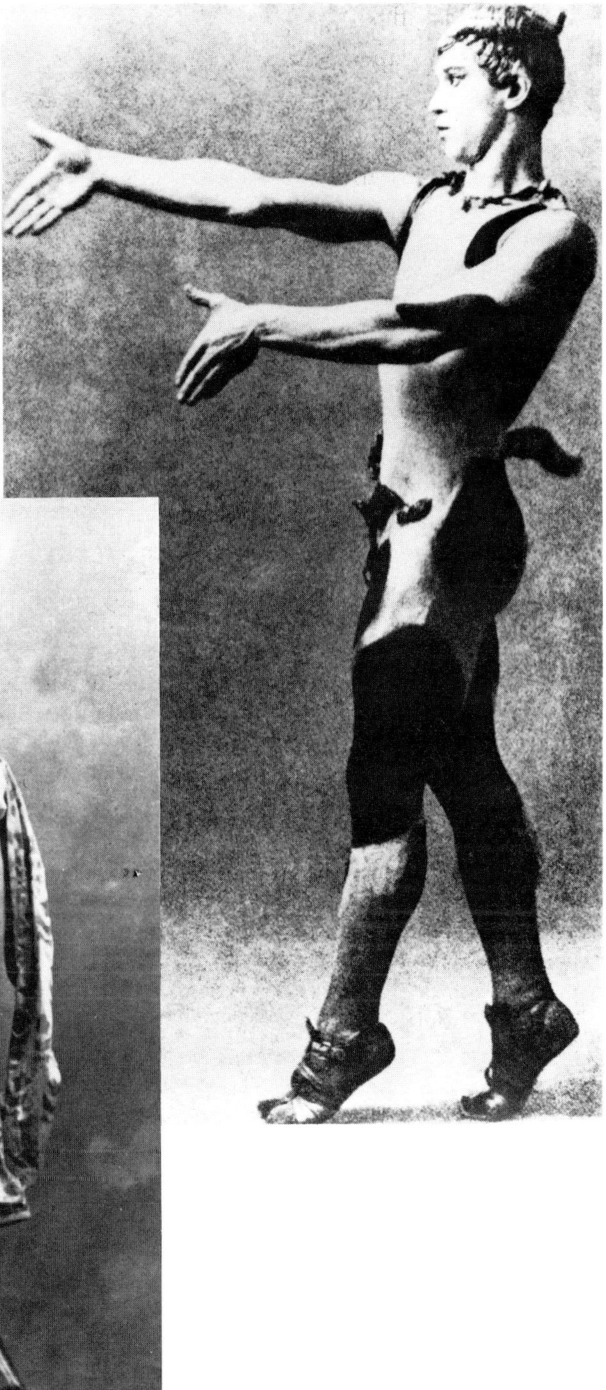

A different image of male dancing emerged with Diaghilev's next protégé and choreographer, Leonid Massine. Massine was not a virtuoso *danseur*, his whole tradition was much more of the dramatic and *demi-caractère* style, and in making roles for himself in his highly successful ballets there emerges a new form of stardom for the male as character dancer. In such early masterpieces as *Le Tricorne*, where Massine was unforgettably the Miller, or in *La Boutique Fantasque*, where he was the boneless and high-kicking Can Can Dancer, he established a new area for male pre-eminence within ballet.

The Diaghilev Ballet during the 1920s brought an entirely fresh image to male dancing, thanks in no small part to Diaghilev's temperamental desire to show off his protégés.

Left: Leonid Massine as the Miller in his own *Le Tricorne*. Massine created the role of the Miller in 1919 as a young man of twenty-four; thirty years later he was still dancing the role with incomparable mastery when he revived the ballet for the Sadler's Wells Ballet at Covent Garden in 1947.

Above: As the Peruvian in his own *Gaieté Parisienne* of 1938 Massine scuttled about the stage with his carpet bags, in a frolic inspired by Offenbach's music. Set in a café, the ballet presented Massine as an innocent abroad, a Peruvian visiting the Paris of the Second Empire.

Thus the young Massine, making roles for himself as he did for the next thirty years, introduced the new strand of *demi-caractère* heroes which began with the Miller in *Le Tricorne* and would continue through the 1930s and 1940s with such roles as the hilarious Peruvian in *Gaieté Parisienne*. Massine continued to dance these roles into the 1950s and was seen to particular effect in similar style in two lurid ballet movies, *The Red Shoes* and *Tales of Hoffmann*.

Diaghilev's two subsequent male stars, Anton Dolin and Serge Lifar, both inspired works intended to display their youthful beauty and physical daring. For the extrovert Dolin *Le Train bleu* epitomised the hero as sporting idol; for the glamorous Lifar there

Anton Dolin as Le Beau Gosse in *Le Train bleu*. Dolin had first appeared with the Diaghilev company in *The Sleeping Princess* in London in 1921 and joined the company as a soloist in 1924. An exceptionally handsome young man, Dolin had vivid temperament and the display elements in *Le Train bleu* were an extract reflection of his physical exuberance, which had provided the first inspiration for Cocteau's libretto.

Serge Lifar was Diaghilev's last male star, and the repertory in which Diaghilev showed him emphasised the extraordinary allure of his youthful beauty. In *Apollo* of 1928, above, he was the personification of the young god. This photograph is a curiosity, since it is a publicity shot which emphasises the beauty of Lifar's legs rather than relating to the choreography. In *La Chatte* (overleaf) he made a triumphant appearance as the hero supported by a group of companions (and the constructivist design by Naum Gabo and Antoine Pevsner speaks very clearly of the period, 1926, when the ballet was staged).

came the more hieratic beauty of *La Chatte*, *Apollo* and *The Prodigal Son*. These last three were choreographed by George Balanchine, obedient to the demands of the Diaghilev aesthetic. But once Balanchine had been given his own artistic freedom, after the death of Diaghilev, his determinedly heterosexual attitude to ballet meant that he celebrated the beauty and gifts of the ballerina more than the male dancer, and it is significant that it was he who discovered and featured the teenage stars of the 1930s, the three 'baby ballerinas', Riabouchinska, Toumanova and Baronova. By the time he went to America, Balanchine's great task was the creation of a classic school and a classic company, the New York City Ballet of today.

Daring Things: a Manly Skill, a Manly Art

I am accused of favouring the boys – the little boys, the big boys, all the boys. And I can not help it, because to my mind when a boy at an ordinary school in any part of England makes the decision to become a ballet dancer, he must have a real vocation. With a girl, it means nothing. Everybody thinks it would be much nicer for her to go to the Royal Ballet School than to become a secretary. But the boys very often make this decision with their fathers and their headmasters in direct opposition and amidst jeers and cries of half the schoolboys. I think it's very touching and I'm out to help all I can. Because there's something else too. Whenever I'm lecturing I always say to people, 'Don't you realise that the history of ballet is the history of the male dancer and the male choreographer?' It has nothing to do with the women, except in a secondary role. It's only when the whole thing's come down to nothing that women become the best pioneer workers. They make the best secretaries, for the same reason, but once ballet's got to a certain level again it's got to be handed back to the men.

Ninette de Valois in *Frederick Ashton* by Zoe Dominic and John Selwyn Gilbert (Harrap, 1971)

When George Balanchine and Lincoln Kirstein set up their school, and subsequently their first company, the general title given to the enterprise was The American Ballet. The nationalism implicit in this had to do with the fundamental reason for Kirstein's invitation to Balanchine – the creation of an authentically American classic tradition. This could be seen as existing in direct opposition to the then very popular and generally accepted idea of '*Russianballet*', which is how Kirstein categorised the ubiquitous and alien image proposed by the Ballet Russe companies that succeeded Diaghilev.

For this company, and for its successor Ballet Caravan, Kirstein among others devised scenarios for a series of ballets which were clearly rooted in the American consciousness and which therefore proposed the male dancer as a typically American figure. *Alma Mater* of 1935 had a scenario by Edward Warburg (one of initial benefactors of the American Ballet and a Harvard man) which poked fun at Yale and Princeton students. Other works of the late 1930s and early 1940s – Lew Christensen's *Pocahontas*, Eugene Loring's *Yankee Clipper*, Christensen's *Filling Station* and Loring's *Billy the Kid* – furthered this quest for American themes and for an American image for the male dancer. Of these ballets *Billy the Kid* still survives in the repertory of American Ballet Theatre. Like many subsequent works it feeds from the legends of the American West and it initiated the image of the dancer as 'cowboy' which was later to receive even greater popularity with Agnes de Mille's *Rodeo* (for Ballet Russe de Monte Carlo) and George Balanchine's *Western Symphony*.

Agnes de Mille, the choreographer of *Rodeo* (which preceded her *Oklahoma!*), is also a writer of exceptional insights, and her volumes of memoirs offer vivid commentary on a remarkable career. In 1942 she was commissioned to create a ballet on a Western theme for the Ballet Russe de Monte Carlo. This was to be *Rodeo*, and the conflicts between male ballet dancers and the physical traditions of the cowboy which were the

Above: *Rouge et Noir* was one of the symphonic ballets which Leonid Massine created during the 1930s for the Ballet Russe companies. With designs by Henri Matisse, it dealt with the struggle between man's spiritual and material forces. Our picture shows Alicia Markova as the heroine surrounded by three of the most important male dancers of the time. André Eglevsky is on the left, Igor Youskevitch is being embraced by Markova, while Frederic Franklin seems to threaten the central pair.

Right: Yurek Shabelevsky was born in Warsaw in 1911 and became one of the greatest stars of the Ballet Russe during the 1930s, renowned for his physical bravura and for his extraordinary good looks which enslaved a generation of gallery girls. More seriously, his performances asserted the power and virility of male dancing.

Page 159: Three men of the London Contemporary Dance Theatre – left to right, Ross McKimm, Robert North, and Micha Bergese – in Robert North's *Troy Game*, first given with this cast in 1974. *Troy Game*, with its all-male cast, was a comment about the jokeyness of athleticism, but its self-mockery also highlighted the exceptional strength of male dancing which LCDT had achieved by that time, and which continues to this day.

André Eglevsky (1911–1977) joined the de Basil Ballet Russe at the age of fourteen. A product of émigré Russian teachers in Paris and London (notably Nicholas Legat), he was celebrated for his technical prowess – not least for pirouettes in which he could slow down his turns, then speed them up again with uncanny control and precision. He is seen here being rehearsed by Mikhail Fokine for *L'Epreuve d'Amour* in 1936, in which he played the hero. After an outstanding career as a dancer he became a distinguished teacher in America.

inspiration for de Mille's choreography are vividly evoked in her first book *Dance to the Piper* (New York 1952). She describes arriving for a first rehearsal and facing the men with this completely new form of movement.

'The riding movements were neither realistic nor imitative. I had worked for a year in London to make them intrinsically beautiful. When performed correctly they suggested the high vigorous emotions of riding. But they were very difficult because the dancer had always to look as though he were propelled by an unseen animal. He hung off balance in the air. He did not jump, he was thrown or wrenched upwards. His feet never touched earth, it was the horses' feet that clattered in the pebbles. The very essence of the movement was shock, spasm and effort.

'Alas, although big boys, they had been trained to move like wind-blown petals. "Raise your arms," I begged them. "You have men's arms, they have striking power, they can control a heavy, moving rope, or the brute furies of an eight-hundred-pound animal."

'Up came the delicate wrists and the curled fingers of the eighteenth-century dandy. "Move from the solar plexus and back," I shouted, "not from the armpit. Think of athletes," I entreated. "Think of throwing a ball, from your feet, from your back, from your guts." But it was a long time since they had thrown balls. They had forgotten. They had not used the ground since they were children except to push away from it. Their arms rose up and down but they themselves looked absolutely stationary.

'"Don't *plier*. Sit your horse," I implored. "There's a difference." But the strain was too much and they relaxed back into bad second position where they felt eminently at home.

'A few Russians lolled on the barre and considered the matter poorly. "It is not dancing," they said. But I had never said it was and I was delighted to excuse them. They picked up their towels and left in haughty silence. The ranks thinned quickly. I had planned to have eighteen men in the cast. I settled for ten. Those that stayed were ready and able.

'For two hours, I rolled on the floor with them, lurched, contorted, jack-knifed, hung suspended and ground my teeth. They groaned and strained. I beat them out in impact, resilience and endurance. I broke them to my handling. I broke them technically, which is where they lived and worshipped.'

The huge success of *Rodeo* was to have a very real effect upon the popular American image of dancing, as well as initiating a new tradition in the American musical which Agnes de Mille inspired with *Oklahoma!* From *Oklahoma!* onwards it was clear that dancing could prove an integral part of the stage action in a musical, being used not as diversion but to further the plot. It also helped break down certain prejudices against the male dancer. He was now to be seen as an American figure. Equally significant in this naturalisation of the male dancer has been the work of Jerome Robbins. A dancer with Ballet Theater, he created a sensation with his first professional work *Fancy Free*. Produced at the Metropolitan Opera House, New York in 1944, this was an inspired example of daily life transferred to the stage with such art that the audience could identify directly and immediately with the characters. The ballet concerned something that was happening at that moment in the streets: three sailors on shore leave chasing two girls. On a hot night in wartime Manhattan this was a common sight, and Robbins preserved its immediacy through a brilliant combination of classical technique and social dance. The three sailors chewed gum, drank beer, played tricks on each other, and chatted up the girls, boasting and showing off in solos which are as vivid as slang. They are totally real, totally recognisable. For the first time an American man in the audience looking at the stage could identify without the remotest embarrassment with three male dancers.

The success of *Fancy Free* was such that its theme became in turn the musical *On the Town* and then a film of the same name. Robbins, in addition to his work for ballet, became one of the great masters of the Broadway musical, and *West Side Story* made the final and most positive statement possible about the importance of dance as the medium for narration, and also suggested how tough urban young could be convincingly shown in dance terms.

Right: Paul Godkin as the Head Wrangler and Jenny Workman as the tomboyish heroine in Agnes de Mille's *Rodeo* with American Ballet Theatre, in the early 1950s.

Below: The Ballet Caravan, one of the precursors of New York City Ballet, staged several ballets aimed at an Americanisation of character ballets. Lew Christensen's *Filling Station*, with its score by Virgil Thomson and designs by Paul Cadmus, was called a 'ballet document'. Its characters were far from the fantasy beings of the Ballet Russe world, as our illustration shows, with Todd Bolender (left) as the State Trouper, Erick Hawkins as the Gangster, Fred Danieli as the Rich Boy and Marie-Jeanne as the Rich Girl. Here were American male dancers interpreting characters from the daily life of the nation.

The three sailors on the town in Jerome Robbins's *Fancy Free*. Were it not for the obviously painted scenery, this could be a photograph taken in Manhattan in 1944. From left to right, Jerome Robbins, John Kriza and Harold Lang – a cast never bettered.

Above left: Gene Kelly and Vera-Ellen in the film of *On The Town*. The twenty-five minutes of Jerome Robbins's *Fancy Free* ballet grew first into a musical and then into a film – although Robbins was not responsible for the film choreography. Gene Kelly made his Broadway success in *Pal Joey* in 1941 and thereafter Hollywood claimed him.

Kelly was also able to stage a ballet for the Paris Opéra, and in such films as *An American in Paris* and *Invitation to the Dance* he did much to extend the possibilities of filmed dance. His most famous film, above right, remains *Singin' in the Rain* in which he was joined by Donald O'Connor.

Left: In the 1954 film *Seven Brides for Seven Brothers* it was the seven brothers who had the lion's share of the dance, choreographed by Michael Kidd, a former dancer with American Ballet Theatre who has gone on to become one of the most influential and distinguished dance directors on Broadway and in Hollywood. In the 'Goin' Courtin'' number Jane Powell is seen with some fine male dancers: from left to right, Marc Platt, Jacques d'Amboise, Matt Mattox, Tommy Rall, Russ Tamblyn, and the actor Jeff Richards.

Above: *West Side Story* remains the ultimate statement in the use of dance as a narrative means in a musical. It was Jerome Robbins who achieved this extraordinary breakthrough, presenting male dancing in terms uncompromisingly contemporary, urban and tough as a stylised manifestation of life on New York's West Side in the 1950s. In this shot from the film of the musical George Chakiris is seen, centre, as Bernardo, the role he created on stage.

Robbins' later career has been largely associated with the New York City Ballet, and in his creations for that company he has consistently enhanced the image of the male dancer. We have but to cite the example of *Dances at a Gathering* and the opportunities it offers to the men.

George Balanchine as guiding genius of the New York City Ballet had always stressed the importance of the female dancer, drawing inspiration from generations of women, and until comparatively late in his career they dominated his greatest ballets. Nevertheless, when offered the talent of the virtuoso Edward Villella, Balanchine could produce exhilarating male choreography, and latterly, with increasing numbers of well-trained male dancers emerging from his school, Balanchine's ballets acknowledged their importance with increasingly important roles.

Though Balanchine paid entirely obvious tribute to the American character of his men in such works as *Stars and Stripes* and *Western Symphony*, it must be said that a more essential portrait of the American male dancer must be that of the less obviously nationalistic figure of the *danseur* in *Square Dance*, where the man's solo is of exceptional beauty; and in the *Baiser de la Fée* Divertimento, where the man has a haunted and poetic variation in which he seems in quest of a lost beloved; or the sportive, austere and passionate portraits of men drawn in *Agon*, that quintessential Balanchine ballet.

Left: Edward Villella in an early performance of Balanchine's *Western Symphony*, and above, as the Prodigal in Balanchine's *The Prodigal Son*, staged by New York City Ballet. A dancer of exceptional brilliance, Villella was also a dramatic artist of rare intensity, as this pose from the first scene of *The Prodigal Son* conveys.

In the last decade of his life, from the time of the Stravinsky Festival of 1972, Balanchine created very important roles for male dancers. For that Stravinsky Festival he made *Symphony in Three Movements* and *Violin Concerto*, in which the men were used as strongly as the women, and *Duo Concertant*, which was a portrait of Peter Martins as the creative artist worshipping his muse. Six years later in *Kammermusik No. 2* he provided a male *corps de ballet* instead of a female one to support his four principals, and in his last major works, *Davidsbündlertänze* and *Mozartiana*, we find him writing as generously and beautifully for men as for women. These roles may not seem overtly 'American' through any externals of appearance or even of step; but they are in their essence very exact portrayals of American men as classic dancers: entirely different from their colleagues and contemporaries in London or Paris or Moscow or Copenhagen, speaking clearly, cleanly and strongly of the classic manner as it was created and refined by Balanchine during his fifty years in the United States. There are, today, many different images of American men proposed by advertising, the cinema, television. One of the truest and most honourable is that revealed by the repertory of the New York City Ballet.

Above left: Kay Mazzo and Peter Martins in the first aria from the Balanchine-Stravinsky *Violin Concerto* of 1972, and above right, Karen von Aroldingen and Jean-Pierre Bonnefous in the second aria. These two duets succeed each other in this masterwork, and the tenderness of the first is matched by a much more abrasive quality in the second, characteristics which have been captured in these two pictures and which convey the emotional life implicit in much of Balanchine's choreography.

Above left: Sean Lavery of the New York City Ballet in John Taras' *Souvenir de Florence*. The clarity and drive of Lavery's dancing are self-evident.

Above: Daniel Duell, a leading dancer of New York City Ballet, in Peter Martins' *Calcium Light Night*, which was Martins' first choreography in 1978. Duell is typical of the new generation of NYCB male dancers: clean and clear in style, his dancing filled with energy.

Left: Douglas Dunn in his own *Foot Rules* of 1979. Dunn is an important 'post-modern' dancer and choreographer whose performances are marked by great physical stamina and imaginative strength. His costume suggests something of the puritanism and anti-theatricality of the latest adventures in modern dance.

Above: Paul Taylor's company in his *Lost, Found and Lost*, which was a dance work – made in 1982 – in which Taylor looked back at some of his early choreographies. Part of the piece's humour came from dressing the men and women exactly alike in suits and head veils.

Left: Merce Cunningham is his own *Travelogue*. Now in his 60s, Merce Cunningham is an indomitable and indefatigable performer, as well as a choreographer, tailoring present performances to a mere appearance as a motivating presence in his works. His *Travelogue* was a typically quirky view of his dance world and no less typically used an artist of the calibre of Robert Rauschenberg as designer.

At the same time that Balanchine was setting about making American ballet, Ninette de Valois and Marie Rambert were putting down the roots for British Ballet. The cosmopolitan touring Ballet Russe companies, with their exciting and fiery male stars, kept ballet in the public eye and perpetuated the idea of male dancing as a 'foreign' and exotic activity. The impression was particularly false in that dancers in the Ballet Russe companies led lives of total isolation from the world. Trapped in incessant touring, and for the most part poorly paid, they had no horizons beyond performance and no hope of any sort of financial security. They were gypsies without homes, or even the basis of a school on which they could rely.

For English dancers one of the most crucial facts was the matter of regular employment guaranteed by Ninette de Valois at Sadler's Wells. Thus her women dancers were sure of a regular if very modest income from one year's end to another, but these salaries were hardly the ideal for a man wishing to marry and settle down. This insecurity, plus the strong prejudice against English boys taking up ballet as a career, meant that male recruitment to the then Vic-Wells school and company was minimal, and inevitably choreographers had to adapt to the material available.

Thus neither with the Vic-Wells nor the Rambert companies could there be much insistence upon virtuosity. Harold Turner, creator of the Blue Boy in Ashton's *Les Patineurs* and the Red Knight in de Valois' *Checkmate*, was the only man with an appreciably strong technique, and these roles remain today evidence of his abilities and a continuing challenge to his heirs. Instead, choreography for the men demanded dramatic sensitivity and a power of theatrical projection which could compel an audience's belief by other than virtuoso means.

For twenty years Robert Helpmann was the star of the Vic-Wells/Sadler's Wells company. A consummate dance actor, he filled out the princely roles with considerable verve; it must be remembered, however, that in the early days of Britain's national ballet the depredations and 'enhancements' of the classic texts had not yet taken place. The prince, as in the days of Gerdt, was a noble figure, required to present the ballerina rather than to display technical bravura. In the ballets made for him by Ashton and de Valois, Helpmann was revealed as an artist of rare romantic passion (thus he was in Ashton's *Apparitions*) and supremely of comic verve – we remember with gratitude his groom in *A Wedding Bouquet*, his drunken delight as Mr O'Reilly in de Valois' *The Prospect Before Us*. His importance to the Sadler's Wells Ballet during the six years of World War II would be hard to overestimate. He led the company in partnership with Margot Fonteyn, and with the departure of Ashton as choreographer and most of the male dancers on war service, he sustained an astounding number of performances and also created a series of ballets which excited considerable interest. These were acutely tailored to the forces which remained to him in these very difficult wartime conditions, and they naturally contained highly effective roles for himself. The three best remembered today are *Comus* (in which he also spoke part of the Milton text), *Hamlet*, a brilliantly effective encapsulation of the play's action as the nightmare dreams of the dying Hamlet, and *Miracle in the Gorbals*, which found Christ returning to the Glasgow slums.

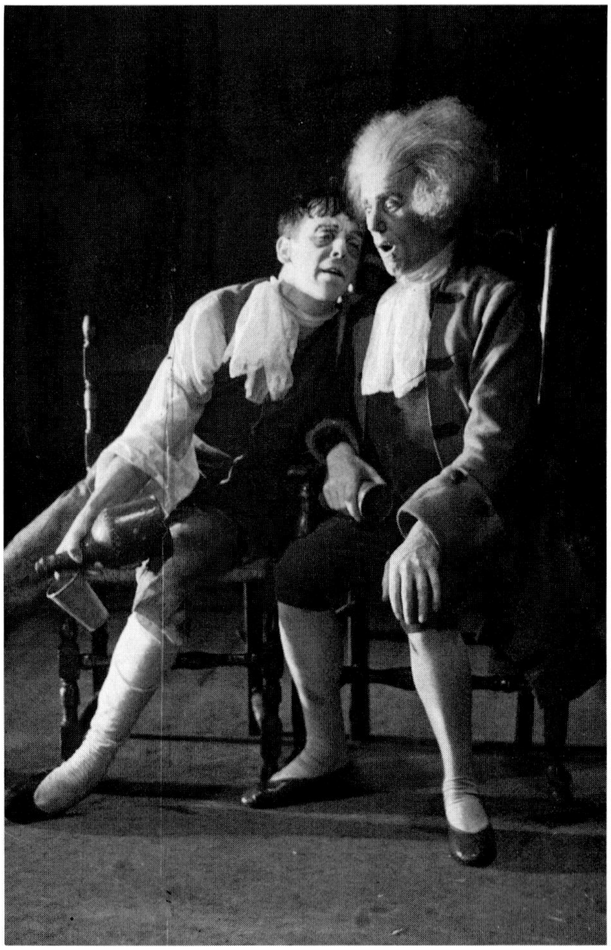

Above: Harold Turner as Harlequin in *Le Carnaval* with the Sadler's Wells Ballet in the 1930s.

Robert Helpmann in two contrasted roles which show the range of this extraordinary dance actor. Above right, he is seen as the bibulous Mr O'Reilly, Manager of the Pantheon, with Claude Newman as Mr Taylor, Manager of the King's Theatre, in Ninette de Valois's *The Prospect Before Us*. The ballet was a lovely joke about theatrical rivalries in London in 1790. It was first produced at Sadler's Wells in 1940 and did much to brighten the gloom of London during the Battle of Britain summer and thereafter. Right, Helpmann is seen in his own *Hamlet*, his encapsulation of Shakespeare's tragedy. This photograph suggests the romantic fever of Helpmann's performance: it is worth noting that, uniquely, Helpmann also appeared as Hamlet in the play.

In the same period with Ballet Rambert a similar situation obtained. With less security than the Vic-Wells, Rambert's choreographers created ballets which made considerable artistic demands upon the male dancers without over-stretching their technical abilities. Thus the important Tudor works of this period, *Jardin aux Lilas* and *Dark Elegies*, call for an emotional and physical sensitivity which has nothing to do with the big guns of technical display, and the later ballets of Frank Staff, Walter Gore and Andrée Howard – all of whom produced major works of art – extended their male dancers as artists (and the artistry of the original casts has never been rivalled) without requiring the virtuosity that was only to be seen in the Ballet Russe companies.

With the war's end and the Sadler's Wells Ballet installed at Covent Garden; with the gradual return of the male dancers from the services; and with an increased enlistment of boys to the company's school, we can see the beginning of a fresh era of male dancing in Britain. At Covent Garden, Ashton's *Symphonic Variations* was a very positive statement about the importance of classic dancing and of new standards for English male dancing. Michael Somes, Brian Shaw and Henry Danton were the three men matched with the company's three superb ballerinas, Margot Fonteyn, Pamela May and Moira Shearer. At no point were the men shown to be inferior. By 1948, with *Scènes de Ballet*, Ashton issued a further challenge of classic elegance to the male dancer and at the same time the second company, the Sadler's Wells Theatre Ballet, had started to show a new generation of English dancers in a new generation of choreography. It was John Cranko's choreography, and David Blair as a wonderfully gifted young dancer, who typify this period at the Wells.

The aspirations and achievements of this time are exactly shown in *Pineapple Poll* and *Harlequin in April*, both of which Cranko made for Blair in 1951. As Captain Belaye in *Poll*, Blair burst on stage as the epitome of dashing and technically brilliant charm. In *Harlequin* he was a vulnerable hero, with another exceptional dancer, Stanley Holden, as his companion Pierrot. These two artists were to be seen at their very best ten years later in Ashton's *La Fille mal gardée* at Covent Garden. In this sunny masterpiece, which represented the greatest bravura challenges every made for British dancers, the heroine Nadia Nerina, a dazzling ballerina, was surrounded by three marvellous and very different male dancers. To David Blair fell the pyrotechnics of the hero's solos; to Holden and to Alexander Grant came the chance to reveal the full range of their comic and dramatic skills in two wonderfully rich character roles. Holden was the first Widow Simone, creator of the famous Clog Dance; Grant was the put-upon Alain whose simplicity is as much pathetic as comic. All three portrayals indicate the increasing powers of British male dancing.

It is from *Fille* onwards that we note the most considerable step forward in English male dancing. The appearance of the Bolshoi Ballet in its first major Western visit to Covent Garden in 1956 had been a revelation, and inevitably an inspiration and a goad to endeavour. The Soviet Ballet had never had any shortage of male dancers, and the aesthetic of ballet in the new Soviet state had very clearly imposed an ideal of heroic strength and brave endeavour upon the man. The choreographies of the 1930s and 1940s

David Blair and Nadia Nerina in the first scene of Ashton's *La Fille mal gardée*, a ballet made to show off their sparkling virtuosity and charm. Blair was the outstanding male dancer of his generation in the Royal Ballet.

The English danseur noble John Gilpin was a star of London Festival Ballet, adored by audiences world-wide for the glamour of his performances and his beautiful technical ease. He is seen here in Harald Lander's *Etudes* in 1959; in this ballet his performances were memorable for their physical brilliance and their great charm. Gilpin died tragically young in 1983 at the age of fifty-three.

had shown the Soviet male dancer as a symbol of Soviet manhood. Ballets as diverse as *The Bronze Horseman, The Fountain of Bakhchisaray, The Flames of Paris* and *Laurencia*, and the new demands imposed upon the male dancer in the classic productions, all stressed a virile energy as an essential quality for the man in ballet. The muscular power and the imposing physique of the Bolshoi's men was in marked contrast to the slimmer, neater figures of Western male dancers; the passionate involvement of the men in the Russian *corps de ballet* was also something invigorating to see. With the Leningrad Kirov Ballet, which made its first appearance in Western Europe in 1961, the emphasis was more on elegance, but the picture of the man was still one of uncompromising masculine dignity. And the arrival of a Kirov dancer, Rudolf Nureyev, in the West following his defection in 1961 was certainly to be the most powerful immediate stimulus to further developments in the range of male dancing, especially in the Royal Ballet which offered him a first base in the West.

It is surely because of the example and the challenge of his exceptional gifts that his contemporaries throughout the Western world found horizons opening in front of them and a stimulus to follow where he so daringly soared.

Above: The men's class in the Bolshoi Theatre. When this photograph was taken the class was being given by Asaf Messerer, great dancer and great pedagogue, and in the front row can be seen three of the leading artists of the Bolshoi Ballet: Yuri Vladimirov, Alexander Godunov (who in 1979 defected from the Bolshoi Ballet on tour in New York), and Maya Plisetskaya, the leading Moscow dancer of her time, and niece of Asaf Messerer, who chose to stretch her powerful technique in the men's class.

Right: Alexander Lapauri (1926–75) as the Khan Girey in *The Fountain of Bakhchisaray*. One of the stars of the Moscow Bolshoi Ballet, Lapauri was a fine example of the Moscow premier danseur of his generation. Tall, very strong, and with a forceful personality, Lapauri could dominate the stage in dramatic roles, and in such concert numbers as the *Moskowski Waltz*, which he danced with his wife, Raissa Struchkova, he demonstrated a virtuosity and strength in partnering impossible to Western artists in his day.

Above: Mikhail Lavrovsky as the slave leader in Yuri Grigorovich's *Spartacus*. *Spartacus* is the definitive statement about Moscow male dancing during the past twenty years. Its demands of huge physical power and impassioned dramatic acting show the Moscow men at their most convincing, and Mikhail Lavrovsky, son of the choreographer Leonid Lavrovsky, gave a performance thrillingly communicative and deeply moving.

Left: Maris Liepa as the villainous Crassus in Grigorovich's *Spartacus*. Grigorovich identified characters in this ballet by a pose or a step, and the vivid curve of Maris Liepa's body suggests the arching leap with which Crassus's cruelty was conveyed to the audience.

Overleaf: Nicolai Fadeyechev of the Bolshoi Ballet in the Prince's solo in Act III of *Swan Lake*. Nothing could more adequately convey the princely grandeur of Fadeyechev's dancing, or the beauty of male classic style, than this picture: harmony, ease and conquest of the air are all implicit.

Above left: Daily class in Leningrad with the late Yuri Soloviev (centre) working at the barre. On the right is another leading dancer of the company, Sergey Vikulov.

Left: This rehearsal picture of the Leningrad Kirov Ballet in a scene from Boris Fenster's *Taras Bulba* shows the men of the company rehearsing a Cossack dance and conveys something of the expansive virility with which this scene was always performed. Anatoly Gridin, an outstanding character dancer, is seen in the centre.

Above: Yuri Soloviev and Alla Sizova in the Blue Bird pas de deux from the third act of *The Sleeping Beauty* as presented by the Leningrad State Kirov Ballet in London in 1961. Soloviev was twenty-one when he was first seen in London and the astounding beauty of his dancing, its classic purity and the sweetness of his personality, made him seem more angel than human. He was a dancer of greatness and in his partnership with Alla Sizova there was a radiance which profoundly affected audiences. He died by his own hand in 1977. His loss is still felt by Soviet ballet, and by everyone who saw him dance.

Rudolf Nureyev shortly after he decided to remain in the West, in a proud, academically pure pose. Twenty years later the magic of his presence was more potent than ever, and he regularly sustained seasons in which he would perform two or three ballets a night.

In Paris in 1982 he was appearing in three Nijinsky roles in an evening: as Petrushka, as the Spirit of the Rose, and here in *L'Après-midi d'un faune*.

Mikhail Baryshnikov is seen above as MacMillan's Romeo, during a guest appearance with the Royal Ballet in which he irradiated the role with his special brilliance and dramatic verve (the photograph shows the marvellous correctness of his classic style). By comparison, he is seen, right, in John McFall's *Follow the Feet* with Robert la Fosse, with American Ballet Theatre in 1983, a romp for two male dancers who try to outdo each other.

Thus, with a new generation of male dancers emerging from ballet schools, and with the dissipation of the old prejudices against men dancing (Nureyev's huge popularity gave resounding importance to the presence of the male dancer) choreographers were increasingly concerned with developing roles to explore the male in ballet.

Frederick Ashton who early in his career relied very much upon his ballerinas, Alicia Markova and Margot Fonteyn, was to be the first to celebrate the emergent generation of British male dancing. He was to write important roles for Christopher Gable, as the Young Painter in *The Two Pigeons*, and for Anthony Dowell as Oberon in *The Dream* and in a succession of roles up to *A Month in the Country*. For Rudolf Nureyev he made his very first solo in the West – the *Poème Tragique* by Skryabin in which the newly defected star roared over the stage like the spirit of liberty itself. Subsequently, he focused Nureyev's romantic fervour as Armand in *Marguerite and Armand*, which was made to sum up the dramatic rapport between Nureyev and Margot Fonteyn. Twenty years later Ashton was also to draw a telling portrait of Mikhail Baryshnikov in *Rhapsody*, where Rakhmaninov's tribute to Paganini is matched by Ashton's appreciation of Baryshnikov's virtuosity.

Anthony Dowell as Siegfried in *Swan Lake* with the Royal Ballet at Covent Garden. Exemplary elegance and beauty of line characterise this beau idéal of the Royal Ballet – a product of its school.

Ashton's heirs, John Cranko and Kenneth MacMillan, were to further the possibilities of male dancing. Cranko it was who first identified David Blair's gifts in a series of *demi-caractère* roles. When he assumed directorship of the Stuttgart Ballet, Cranko's concern was to create both a repertory and an ensemble, and with such fine male dancers as Ray Barra, Richard Cragun and Egon Madsen he produced works which, in the best traditions of the relationship between a dancer and a choreographer, extended and confirmed their stage identity. Ray Barra he made his Romeo; Cragun he identified to the world as high-soaring virtuoso and a most potent dramatic player as Petruchio in *The Taming of the Shrew* and in *Opus 1*, and he also acted as catalyst for the unique partnership of Cragun with Marcia Haydée; Madsen he presented as a romantic hero, Lensky in *Onegin*, and an uproarious comedian in *Jeu de Cartes*. Something of the essential relationship between a choreographer and his dancers is very clearly to be sensed in Cranko's *Initials R.B.M.E.* which explores the interdependence of creator and interpreters – the initials being those of the Christian names of four of his leading dancers. For the two males involved – Richard Cragun and Egon Madsen (the R and E of the title) – the ballet remains a loving portrait and commentary upon their identity as artists and as vital members of Cranko's Stuttgart 'family'.

With Kenneth MacMillan we enter the realm where classic ballet is allied to searching inquiries into psychological motivation. An elegant classical dancer, from the very beginnings of his career MacMillan created roles of real importance for men – we recall the muscular brilliance of the late Donald Britton in *Danses Concertantes*, MacMillan's first commissioned ballet; the poetic elegance of Donald MacLeary as the hero in *Le Baiser de la Feé*; the sensitivity of Christopher Gable as the boy in *The Invitation*. But it is in his full-length ballets, a genre traditionally dominated by the ballerina, that MacMillan has made an especially potent image for the male dancer.

His first big ballet was *Romeo and Juliet*, and though the motor that drives the ballet is the passionate and positive character of Juliet as made for that most passionate and positive ballerina, Lynn Seymour, Romeo (a role created for Christopher Gable) and his companions Mercutio and Benvolio (David Blair and Anthony Dowell) and Tybalt (Desmond Doyle, bitter and dominating) were strongly defined characters. A succeeding full-length work, *Anastasia*, was very much concerned with the caracter of its heroine, but with *Manon*, which MacMillan made in 1974, the innocently voluptuous heroine is surrounded by three admirably contrasted male roles: her scheming and immoral brother Lescaut, her besotted lover Des Grieux, and the wealthy G.M. who buys her. Lescaut was created for David Wall, a dancer-actor of vivid abilities, and MacMillan established the vulpine identity of the character at curtain-rise when we see Lescaut seated on the stage, draped in a black cloak and peering like a predator from under his hat at the corrupt world of Paris during the Régence. Lescaut moves through the ballet like Manon's evil genius, but he is also revealed as a character of sardonic charm, and to him and his mistress MacMillan gives the wonderful comic invention of a *pas de deux* in which the drunken Lescaut *just* managed to catch and hold his lady friend before collapsing in a stupor at her feet. Des Grieux was written for Anthony Dowell,

Egon Madsen, a Danish-born dancer, made his career with the Stuttgart Ballet, and was one of the team of artists whose development was shaped by John Cranko. His roles included both romantic heroes and eccentric comedy, and he is seen, right, as the ludicrous Gremio, victim of a monster cold in the head, in Cranko's *Taming of the Shrew*. Below, he is the incarnation of romantic passion as Armand Duval, with, in the background, Marcia Haydée as Marguerite Gautier, in John Neumeier's *Lady of the Camellias*, created for the Stuttgart Ballet.

Opposite: Richard Cragun soaring above the cast as Petruchio in John Cranko's *The Taming of the Shrew* with Marcia Haydée as Katherine standing menacingly centre stage back in bridal attire. Cragun's performance is a marvellous compendium of humour and bravura. Cranko, typically, made fine use of Cragun's technical prowess – he happily performs triple air turns as Petruchio – when he created *Shrew* for the Stuttgart Ballet in 1969.

Above: Christopher Gable and Lynn Seymour, in the roles made for them by Kenneth MacMillan, as the young lovers in *Romeo and Juliet* with the Royal Ballet in 1965. Though Juliet is the motive force in the ballet, MacMillan's choreography was generous in providing several excellent male roles. Christopher Gable has not been equalled in the youthful charm of his portrayal. He retired from dancing early and has subsequently made a very distinguished career as an actor and also as a teacher.

Right: David Blair as Mercutio in Kenneth MacMillan's *Romeo and Juliet*. This 'still' from the Rank Organisation film of the ballet captures Mercutio's joie de vivre and Blair's charm in demi-caractère roles.

whose partnership with Antoinette Sibley, the Manon of the first performance, has been of great importance to the Royal Ballet. Dowell, the supreme example of English classic elegance in dance, filled out his role with a romantic innocence, and the purity of his dancing was exactly matched by that of Sibley in their *pas de deux*. It is some comment upon the potential of these two male roles and of their interpreters that in subsequent performances, with Lynn Seymour as Manon, Dowell and Wall exchanged roles, and Dowell as Lescaut joined Seymour in creating an impression of incestuous self-absorption between brother and sister which excluded everybody else from their private world and private destinies, while David Wall brought a temperamental liveliness which focused sharply upon Des Grieux's obsession for the worthless Manon.

The role of G.M. was created for Derek Rencher, and in it we see the clarity and detail of playing which have also made his performances memorable in such ballets as *Anastasia*, where he was Tsar Nicholas II, and Ashton's *Enigma Variations* in which he seemed Elgar come to life.

Four years after *Manon* MacMillan created *Mayerling*, and with it what is arguably the most demanding role yet made for a male dancer in Western ballet. The action is concerned with the death in the hunting lodge at Mayerling in 1889 of Archduke Rudolf, heir to the Austro-Hungarian throne, and of Maria Vetsera, his mistress of two weeks. The ballet is important on many accounts, not least for its demands upon the male dancer, but no less significant is its desire to use the fact of history rather than any form of dramatic fiction to provide the inspiration for choreography. Hence Rudolf is a 'real' character, and Kenneth MacMillan and his scenarist Gillian Freeman were at pains to de-romanticise the soggy love story proposed by the cinema and literary convention. Their concern was with the historical truth of Rudolf – a compulsive womaniser; a prince involved in a political separatist movement; a young man rejected by his mother; and finally a morphinomaniac whose sexual fantasies involved an obsession with guns – and from these tragic and unsavoury elements to establish a drama which would explain and perhaps justify the sad chronicle of his life. It was David Wall who offered the inspiration of that strong technique and remarkable dramatic sensitivity which helped shape the tremendous role that MacMillan made for him. It is some tribute to the power of Wall's performance and MacMillan's choreography that the character's progressive degradation, which is shown in harrowing detail, wins the entire sympathy of the audience. Wall's is a great creation. (It is worth noting that the action of the ballet is, in fact, a bizarre inversion of the *Swan Lake* story.) But it is a comment upon the impressive power of the Royal Ballet's male dancers that the role has subsequently been played and superbly explored by three other male dancers: Wayne Eagling, Stephen Jefferies and Derek Deane. Their readings have been markedly different but wholly convincing. This in itself is the best criterion of the quality of MacMillan's choreographic imagination.

The choreographies of Ashton, Cranko and MacMillan are rooted in the classic academic tradition, but a significant development in dance in the past two decades has been a cross-fertilisation between classical ballet and the attitudes of contemporary dance. A leading and influential exponent of this mixed marriage has been Glen Tetley,

Above: David Wall as Crown Prince Rudolf in Kenneth MacMillan's *Mayerling*. This portrait by Anthony Crickmay well conveys the brooding unhappiness of Rudolf and also Wall's extraordinary ability to invest the character with potent life.

Right: Christopher Bruce in Glen Tetley's *Pierrot Lunaire*. Bruce's interpretation of the title-role was remarkably powerful in its expressive force – and it has been happily captured on television film. Pierrot is seen here being manipulated like a puppet by Columbine and Brighella.

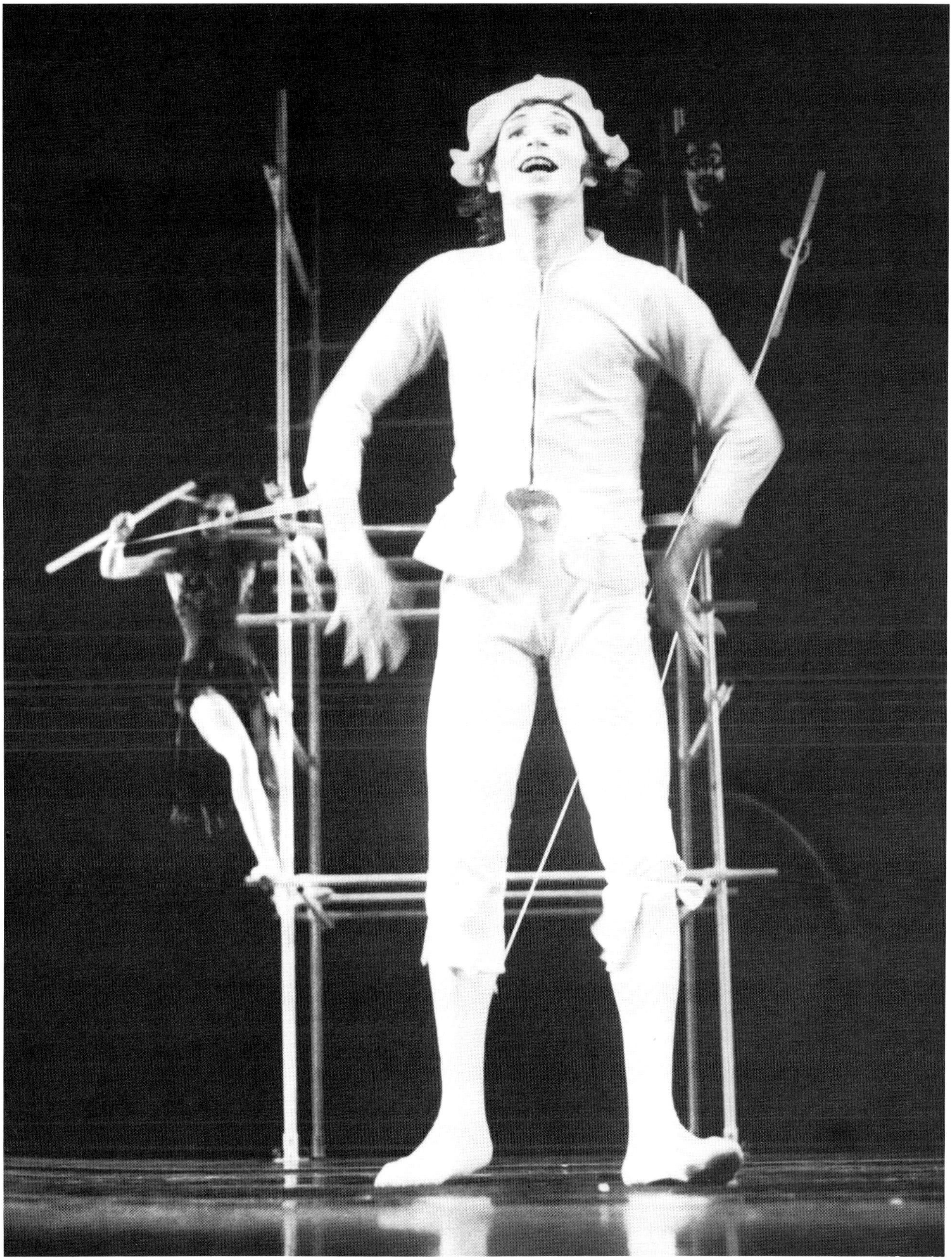

American-born but most active in Europe. Tetley's initial training was both in ballet and modern dance. His first choreographic success was *Pierrot Lunaire*, staged in New York in 1962. Inspired by Schoenberg's score, it was concerned with the eternal innocent, Pierrot, subjected to the mockery and humiliations of the worldly Columbine and the brutally experienced Brighella. The identities of these *Commedia dell' arte* figures were merely symbolic. Tetley's theme was the disclosure of how innocence can reconcile itself to the cruelties of the world, and in the role of Pierrot Tetley created a persuasive portrait of the new male dancer. It is a role which has been danced by Tetley himself and by many other fine artists, notably the Royal Danish Ballet's Niels Kehlet and Ballet Rambert's Christopher Bruce, whose performances have shown a heroic pathos. In many of his subsequent ballets Tetley has been concerned with the social and sexual tensions of modern man, and his choreographies have encouraged male dancers to a greater frankness of expression and have been markedly influential in shaping a style which has been adopted by later choreographers.

It was Glen Tetley who first helped fix the image of Ballet Rambert when the company was re-formed in 1967, and in the choreographies which Christopher Bruce subsequently created for Rambert we can see how he moved on from the position established by Tetley and made ballets – *Black Angels*, *Cruel Garden* among them – which again extended the emotional range for the male dancer.

At the same time that Ballet Rambert was being reshaped in a contemporary mould, mainstream American modern dance was introduced into Britain when Robert Cohan, a distinguished dancer with Martha Graham, was invited by Robin Howard to set up a school and develop a company in London. It had been a tradition established in America that men could come late to contemporary dance and still make impressive careers (Cohan had started dancing after Army service and had swiftly achieved eminence in the Graham troupe). Thus in London many young men were inspired to take up dance training at an age when it would have been impossible for them to become ballet dancers, and the early health of the London Contemporary Dance Company and its School reflected the availability of young men who were not subjected to the sorts of prejudice which would have inhibited them from ever studying ballet.

There resulted from this, and from the proselytising zeal of the London Contemporary Dance organisation, a considerable interest among young men and schoolboys in the possibility of dance careers. Times had changed. The old inhibitions against dance as a manly art were being eroded (in ballet, too, where there was impressive recruitment of boys for the Royal Ballet School) and the choreographies with which Robert Cohan now set about building an identity for the London Contemporary Dance School and Company, stressed the importance of the male dancer. The present excellence of the male contingent in the London Contemporary Dance Company, led by such fine artists as Patrick Harding-Irmer, and the highly promising young men who emerge each year from the School, will suggest better than any words of ours that the male dancer is unashamedly and essentially part of the contemporary dance scene.

As in the United States, the expansion of contemporary dance has depended upon splits and secessions from a parent company. In Britain, graduates from the London Contemporary Dance School have made a vital contribution to an increased public awareness of dance. Micha Bergese has formed his own company, *Mantis*; Ross McKimm and Anthony van Laast have worked widely as teachers and choreographers; Richard Alston and Robert North are now respectively chief choreographer and artistic director of Ballet Rambert, and their ballets have been seen with companies throughout the world. From Robert North has come one of the most popular recent views of the male dancer. His *Troy Game* was originally created for London Contemporary Dance Theatre in 1974. Inspired by the rhythms of Brazilian music it proposes male dancers as ultra-macho athletes whose activities often teeter upon self-mockery and physical disaster. As danced by companies as diverse as the Royal Ballet and the Dance Theatre of Harlem it offers a lot of muscular humour and an undeniably strong image of male dancing. So, in a much purer way, does Robert Cohan's *Class* which is a choreographed study of the essential training for a contemporary dancer. In it, men and woman perform the exercises that are the basis of their daily class routine, and in writing for the men Cohan stresses both the controlled vigour and the powerful space-devouring energies that are necessary for a male dancer today.

The men of London Contemporary Dance Theatre are a magnificent ensemble. Their powerful style reflects the development of Graham training which has been achieved by Robert Cohan over a period of 15 years. This technique and the men's bravura is celebrated in Cohan's *Class*.

There is in Europe one company which has throughout its quarter-century of existence consistently proclaimed the importance of the male dancer. This is the Ballet du XXème Siècle, based in Brussels, and the creative expression of the dance ideals of Maurice Béjart. Born in Marseille in 1928, Béjart started as a classical dancer, appearing with a variety of traditional troupes, but by the mid 1950s he had organised his own ensemble dedicated to a more contemporary image, through use of *musique concrète* and modern design. In 1959 he became director of the ballet company at the Théâtre Royal de la Monnaie, the Brussels opera house, and from this there emerged the Ballet du XXème Siècle. Starting with a sensational staging of Stravinsky's *Le Sacre du Printemps*, Béjart has produced a series of monumental spectacles, large in scale and often very complex in their theorising (it is no accident that Béjart is the son of the philosopher Gaston Berger). In such ballets as *Nijinsky, Clown of God*; *Trionfi*; Beethoven's *Ninth Symphony*; *Bhakti*; *Golestan, A Mass for the Present Time*, and *Light* (1982) Béjart has aimed for a form of communication with vast audiences, seeking an immediate emotional response from his public irrespective of any existing boundaries of 'opera house' mentality of age or class. He has been especially successful in appealing to a young audience who would not otherwise choose to venture into an opera house. As we have indicated, Béjart has done much to free and enhance the image of the male dancer on the stage, and in a conversation with the American writer John Gruen, published in *The Private World of Ballet* (Viking Press, New York, 1975) Béjart said:

'As for my celebrating the male dancer rather than the female dancer, I do this because I have come to realise that our first dancing was folk dancing, where the real dancers were always the males – they were the more important element of the dance. In early folk dancing, the women were merely beautiful – they followed, they helped. I mean, look at Russian folk dancing. The men dance, and the women go around with handkerchiefs. In Japanese dancing, it's always the man. The same in African dancing. In Africa, women are often not allowed to dance or even appear. Look at the American Indian dances. They were and are always executed by the males. And so, I found out that the origin of dancing was built for the power of the man. Women come to add beauty and femininity.'

There results from this viewpoint a choreographic manner and choreographic material which offer a particular view of the man on stage. It is athletic, often highly emotional. His male stars have included Paolo Bortoluzzi and Jorge Donn (who has created many leading roles for Béjart), and with a company exceptionally strong in male soloists Béjart offers his public works which can indeed be said to glorify the male dancer within the severe limits of Béjartian choreography. There is an implicit sensuality which has more to do with musculature than dance invention. But Béjart explains this:

'For me, ballet is an art form that is deeply connected to two things: cinema and sport. . . . I believe that ballet has much to learn from the cinema – from the way it moves. And ballet has much to learn from sport, because sport, like ballet, is a body performance. Dancers do daring things. They jump, have extensions, difficult movements, power. My own choreography comes from the connection and relationship to

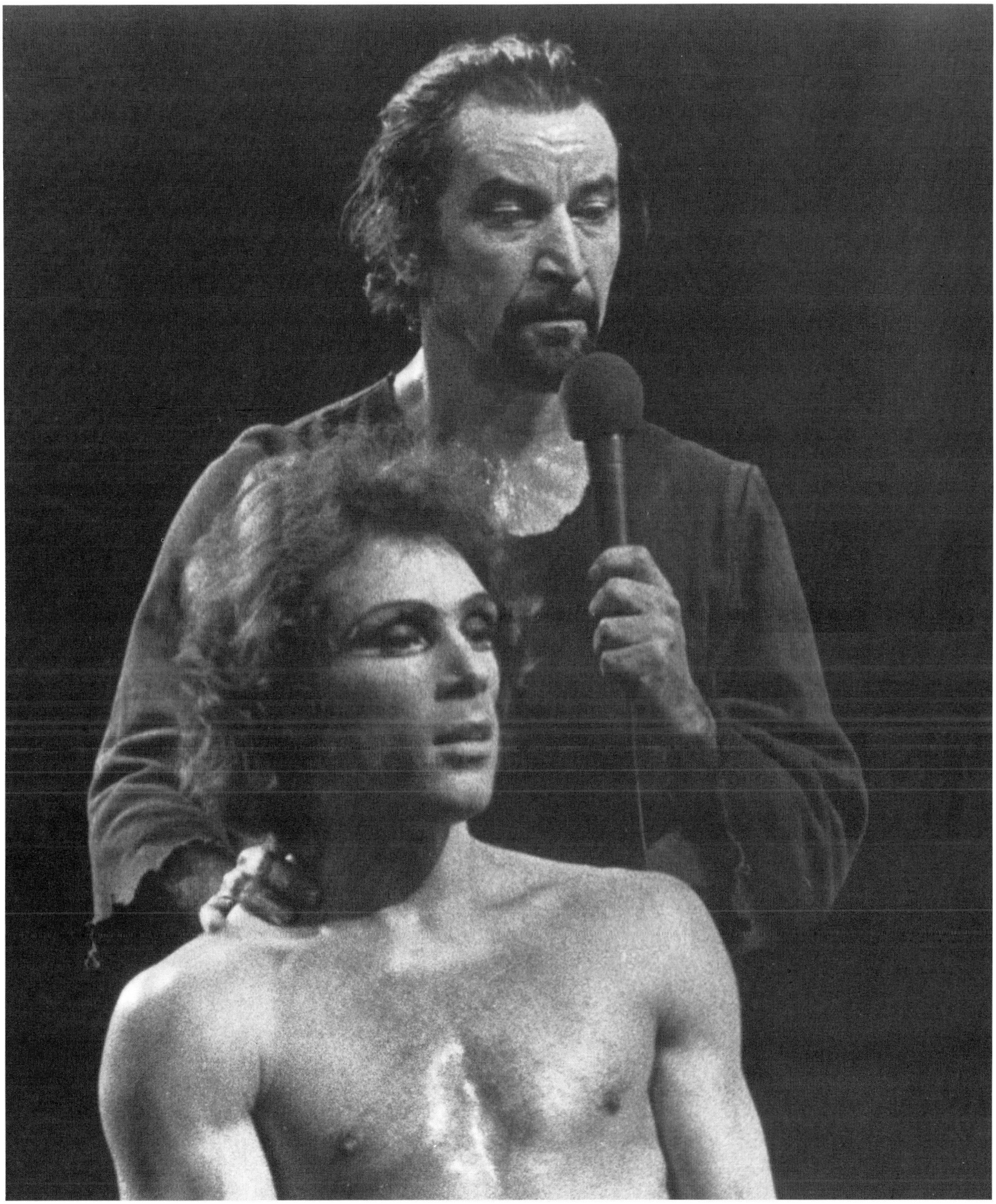

Maurice Béjart and Jorge Donn in *Notre Faust*, in which Béjart was a guiding spirit as well as choreographer, and is seen here with Jorge Donn who has been his favourite interpreter for many years.

Jorge Donn in *Amor di Poeta* by Maurice Béjart. This photograph indicates something of the shock treatment which Béjart uses to capture his audiences' attention. The male dancer is turned into a figure to outrage convention, with a raucous theatricality which owes little to the traditional presentation of the man on the dance-stage.

these two great arts. Also – I like my ballets to be sexy. Because it is part of nature, and I am a primitive. I am not a civilised man. Deep inside I am savage. That is why civilised people often hate me and my work so much.'

The inspiration offered by Maurice Béjart to his dancers is very real – one of the most obvious qualities of the Ballet du XXème Siècle is the sense of corporate endeavour and mutual trust which is generated by the ensemble, and this the audience responds to as it responds to the extreme sense of dedication to the matter in hand which is always evident in a performance by the company. It is this which gives the presentation of works as different as Béjart's *Firebird* or his *Magic Flute* their immediacy, and whatever lack of sympathy the observer may feel for Béjart's dances, his dancers win unqualified respect.

The nature of Béjart's influence over his dancers is typified by Jorge Donn's commentary in *The Private World of Ballet*. 'From the very beginning I knew he would be my one great teacher. I also knew that if one found such a person, one would have to give oneself to him completely. I started in the corps, and little by little, went on to dance larger roles. All I know is that when you dance for Béjart, you are dancing for something important. It's not merely a matter of doing something with one's legs and feet, or to possess a pretty smile. Béjart is not only a great choreographer – he is a great philosopher. There are few people like that in the world. He has given his life to the dance, and he has raised the dance to new heights.'

It is this enthusiasm for dance, and the establishing of a new image for the male dancer, that has also been an interesting aspect of ballet in Holland, where the postwar years saw the emergence of a lively ballet tradition. With few hang-ups about a classical past, and through the work of three young Dutch choreographers – Hans van Manen, Rudi van Dantzig and Toer van Schayk – and with the participation of the American Glen Tetley, the Nederlands Dans Theater and the National Ballet of Holland started on a period of considerable creativity. In the 1960s and 1970s both companies were prepared to experiment, and the 'permissive' society and the increasingly politicised nature of the arts are reflected in their repertories. There was often a frankness about relationships in the Dutch choreography of the time – from the nudity seen in the Tetley/van Manen *Mutations* to the homosexuality of *Monument for a Dead Boy* – which helped extend the range of roles open to the male dancer. The man was no longer a prince, or a conventional and slightly stuffy danseur: he was neurotic, and freed from many of the physical conventions which still acted as contraints on the men in the audience who were watching him. He was the male dancer as apostle of freedom and sexual honesty.

The most recent and significant development in Dutch ballet has been the work of Jiři Kyliàn, a Czech-born choreographer, with Nederlands Dans Theater. In Kyliàn's ballets the observer is first aware of the high expenditure of energy that is called upon from the dancers. Men and women often dash, race and tear over the stage; here is an undifferentiated athleticism, an unspecified emotionalism, which many audiences find attractive and moving, cast in the boldly physical terms of Kyliàn's style. One of his

John Neumeier's *Illusions – Like Swan Lake* is a highly individual view of the ballet classic, which turns the traditional hero Siegfried into Ludwig of Bavaria and also finds parallels between Ludwig's homosexuality and that of Tchaikovsky. In the ballet the King is haunted by a figure in black who is both his fate and his beloved, and our illustration shows part of the final pas de deux, with Ivan Liska as the figure in black and François Klaus as Ludwig.

most successful ballets is written for an all-male cast: *The Soldiers' Mass*, set to a Martinů score, is a portrait of men in battle. Twelve soldiers are shown in uniform, and the dance action presents them as victims not only of battle but also of the tensions and fears that must attend any man in war. This is a highly contemporary view of the male dancer, and as with every Kyliàn piece it demands intense physical concentration and maximum effort.

Kyliàn's troupe, like Béjart's, impresses its audience with a dedicated exposure of its choreographer's intentions, and so, too, do the artists of the Hamburg Ballet respond to the wishes of their choreographer and director, John Neumeier. In his own choreographies, and in his new versions of the traditional classics, Neumeier helps reassert the renewed importance of the male dancer for European audiences. His *Swan Lake* and his *Sleeping Beauty* are innovatory stagings which reflect a desire to show the prince as justification for the action. In *The Sleeping Beauty* a young man in jeans, later to become the prince, observes the action of the ballet from the very beginning; in *Illusions – Like Swan Lake* the central figure of Siegfried also becomes Ludwig of Bavaria. In his own ballets Neumeier stresses the importance of the male dancer, and he explores the psychological and physical tensions of his heroes in such varied works as *Hamlet Connotations* and *The Legend of Joseph*, as in his *Meyerbeer/Schumann* and *Don Juan*.

In the works of the many and varied choreographers whom we have cited, we can see today how the male dancer is called upon to explore every aspect of his identity as technician and as interpretative artist. In the theatre, as in social dance, and in such extreme forms of youth dance as 'slamming', with its aggressive booted force, or 'breaking', that street-born whirling and spinning whereby teenagers find release from urban disappointment and frustration, men are dancing with an honesty and an assurance they have not known for nearly two centuries. The one-time dominance of the ballerina has been replaced by a concern – even an over-riding concern – for the male artist. As Dame Margot Fonteyn summed up the situation in her television series *The Magic of the Dance*: 'the era of the ballerina is over'.

Acknowledgements

Picture Credits

AMERICAN BALLET THEATRE pages 101, 165; H. BADEKOW page 202; BARNABY'S PICTURE LIBRARY page 117 top; BARRATTS PHOTO PRESS page 39 top; BBC ENTERPRISES pages 104 top, 197; BBC HULTON PICTURE LIBRARY pages 13 right, 16, 26, 27 top right, 28 bottom right, 34, 45 top right, 114 all photos, 115 bottom left, 116 top and bottom right, 156 left, 158 & 174 bottom right; BEJART'S BALLET OF THE XXth CENTURY pages 215, 216; BIBLIOTHEQUE NATIONALE, PARIS pages 9, 12, & 140 left; JOHN BLOMFIELD page 92; MICHEL BOURGUET pages 40 top, 62 & 80/81; JOE BULAITIS PHOTOGRAPHY page 63; CAMERA PRESS LTD/PUCCIANO page 65; DANIEL CANDE page 185; STEVEN CARAS page 139; CLARKE-CRISP COLLECTION pages 18, 19, 24 both, 25 both, 29 top, 31 both, 36, 37, 45 left & bottom right, 46 top, 48, 49, 51 both, 53 left, 73 left, 76, 85, 87 bottom, 88, 89, 90, 106, 109, 120 top left & right, 128 left, 130 both, 131, 132, 140 right, 144 right, 145, 148 both, 149 both, 151, 152, 153 both, 154, 155 both, 157, right, 161 bottom, 164 bottom, 166 all photos, 172 bottom, 178 bottom; CONSTANTINE page 87 top; ANTHONY CRICKMAY title page and pages 57, 59, 73 right, 77 bottom, 97, 98 both, 99 both, 122, 159, 169, 182 bottom, 183, 191, 194, 195; MERCE CUNNINGHAM DANCE CO page 82 top; JOHN CURRY THEATRE OF SKATING page 64; DANCE PERSPECTIVES FOUNDATION/VERA KRASOVSKAYA COLLECTION, LENINGRAD page 144 left; FREDERIKA DAVIS page 179 bottom; ZOE DOMINIC pages 94 top, 95; WILLIAM DUPONT page 42; RICHARD FARLEY pages 74, 75, 100 bottom, 105, 110 both; FRED FEHL pages 112 & 133 both; FITZWILLIAM MUSEUM, CAMBRIDGE page 21 right; CAROL HALEBIAN page 119 bottom; H. A. HALLAS page 120 bottom; HARPER & ROW INC page 157 left, from *Diaghilev and the Ballets Russes* by Boris Kochno, MIKE HUMPHREY page 186; JOHN R. JOHNSEN pages 136 & 138; KEYSTONE/CENTRAL PRESS pages 107 & 115 top right; KEYSTONE/FOX PHOTOS page 115 bottom right; HANNES KILIAN page 190 top; KOBAL COLLECTION page 46 bottom; SERGE LIDO page 39 bottom; JACQUES LOW pages 40 bottom & 41; MUSEUM OF THE CITY OF NEW YORK page 27 top left and bottom right, 142; MUSEUM OF MODERN ART, NEW YORK page 141 'Cake Walk'. The American minstrels Williams and Walker in their famous cakewalk. New York (1890?). Watercolour 22″ × 22″. Collection, the Museum of Modern Art, New York. Given anonymously; RIGMOR MYDTSKOV pages 132 top & 135; NEW YORK CITY BALLET pages 113, 170 both & 171 right; NEW YORK PUBLIC LIBRARY AT LINCOLN CENTRE page 50; NOVOSTI PRESS AGENCY pages 53 right, 54, 61, 72, 147, 178 top, 179 top, 182 top; ANDREW OXENHAM page 100 left; RANK ORGANISATION pages 116 left & 192 bottom; REX FEATURES LTD page 117 bottom; H. ROGER VIOLLET pages 14, 21 left, 28 top and bottom left, 38, 100 right (Lipnitzki) & 162 (Lipnitzki); ROY ROUND page 192 top; SCHOOL OF AMERICAN BALLET/PHOTOS PAUL KOLNIK pages 68, 69, 70 & 71; S.C.R. pages 180/181; MAURICE SEYMOUR page 161; DONALD SOUTHERN page 93; LESLIE E. SPATT pages 103, 188 & 190 bottom; MARTHA SWOPE 29 bottom, 78, 94 bottom, 113, 137 both, 168, 170 (both), 171 top left & 187; PAUL TAYLOR DANCE FOUNDATION INC pages 77 top & 172 top; NATHANIEL TILESTON pages 79 & 171 bottom left; THEATRE MUSEUM, VICTORIA AND ALBERT MUSEUM pages 11, 15, 17, 23 and photos by GORDON ANTHONY pages 109 left, 166, 174 top left; J. W. DEBENHAM page 174 top right, and photos by HOUSTON ROGERS pages 55, 176 & 184; TIMES NEWSPAPERS LTD/PHOTO SALLY SOAMES page 82 bottom; TWYLA THARP DANCE FOUNDATION INC page 121; UNITED ARTISTS page 167; JACK VARTOOGIAN pages 118 & 119 top; VICTORIA AND ALBERT MUSEUM page 13 left; VON HAVEN PRESS page 134; G. B. L. WILSON pages 43, 110 top & 177; ROGER WOOD page 164 top.

Index

Italic numerals refer to pictures

BALLETS